Animal Heads Coloring Book

Detailed Animal Head Designs Coloring Book

Sandra Bacon

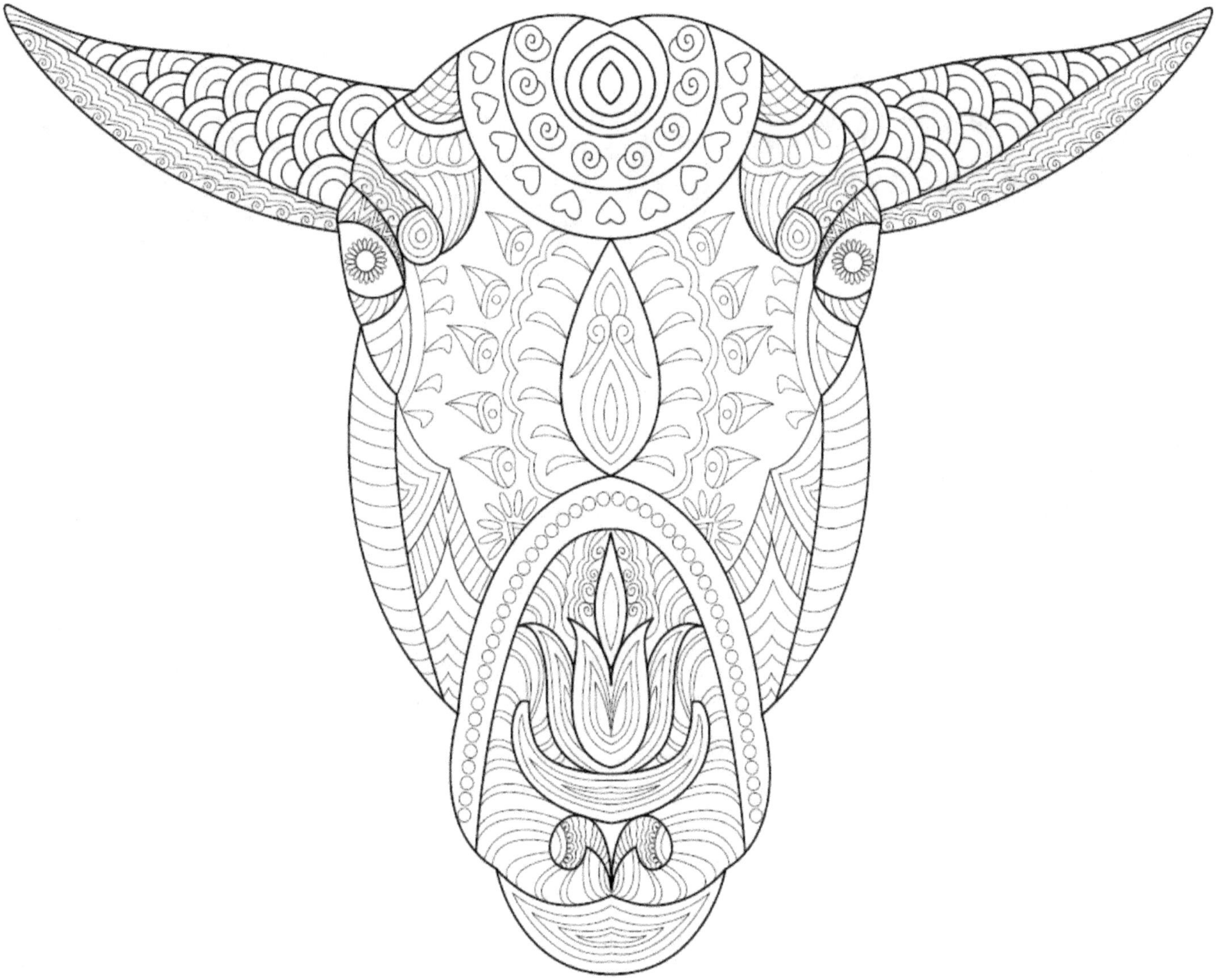

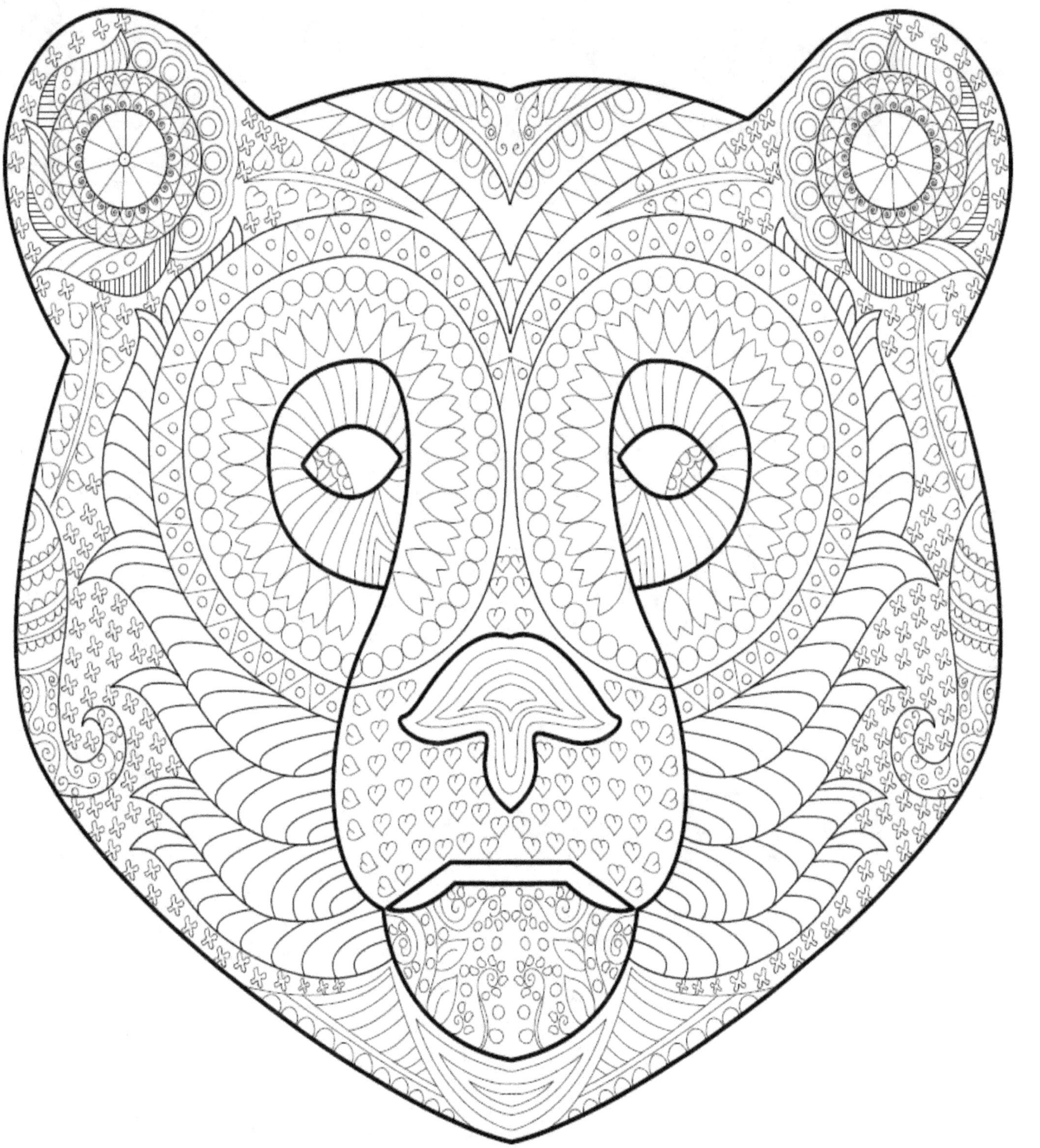

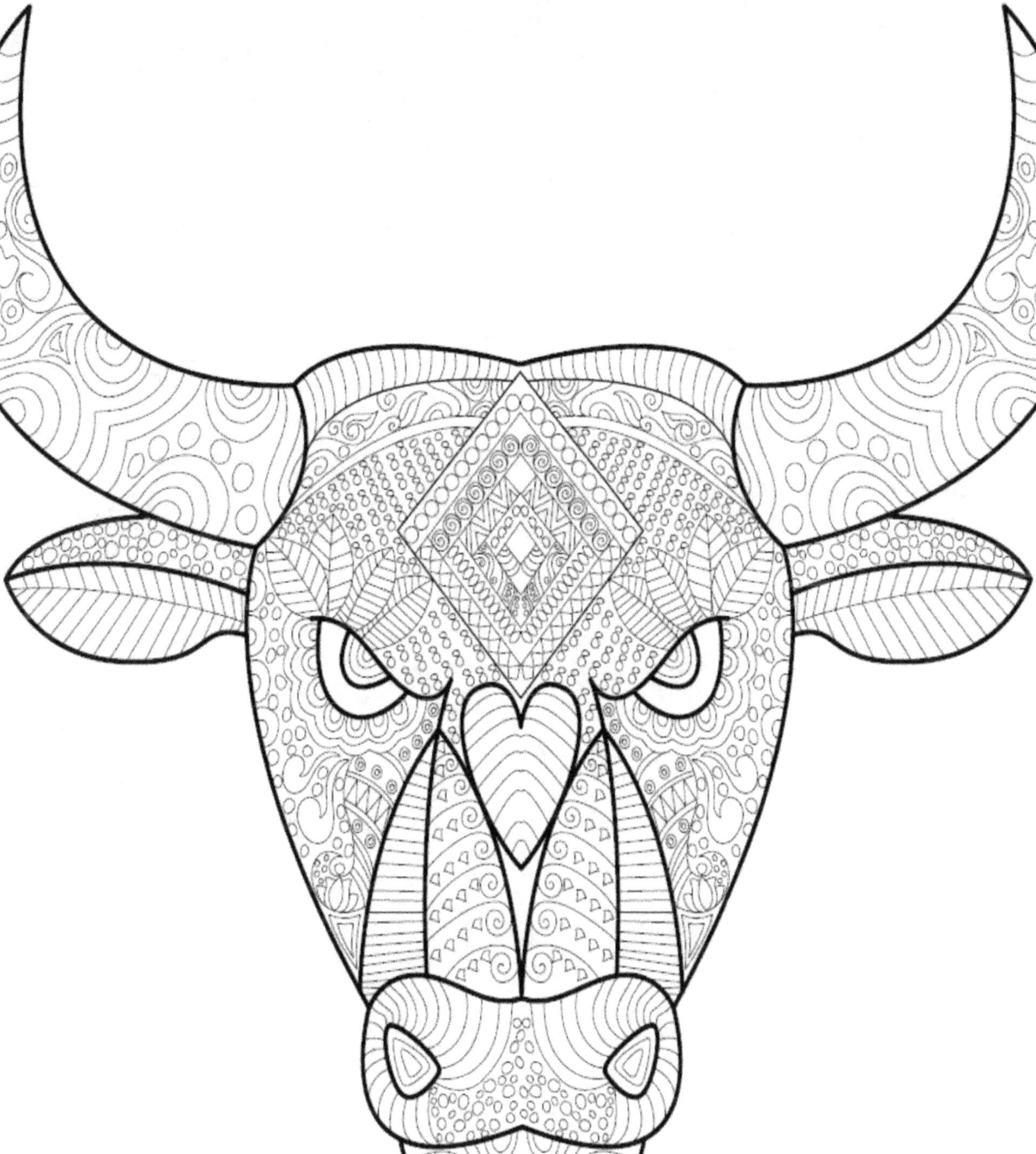

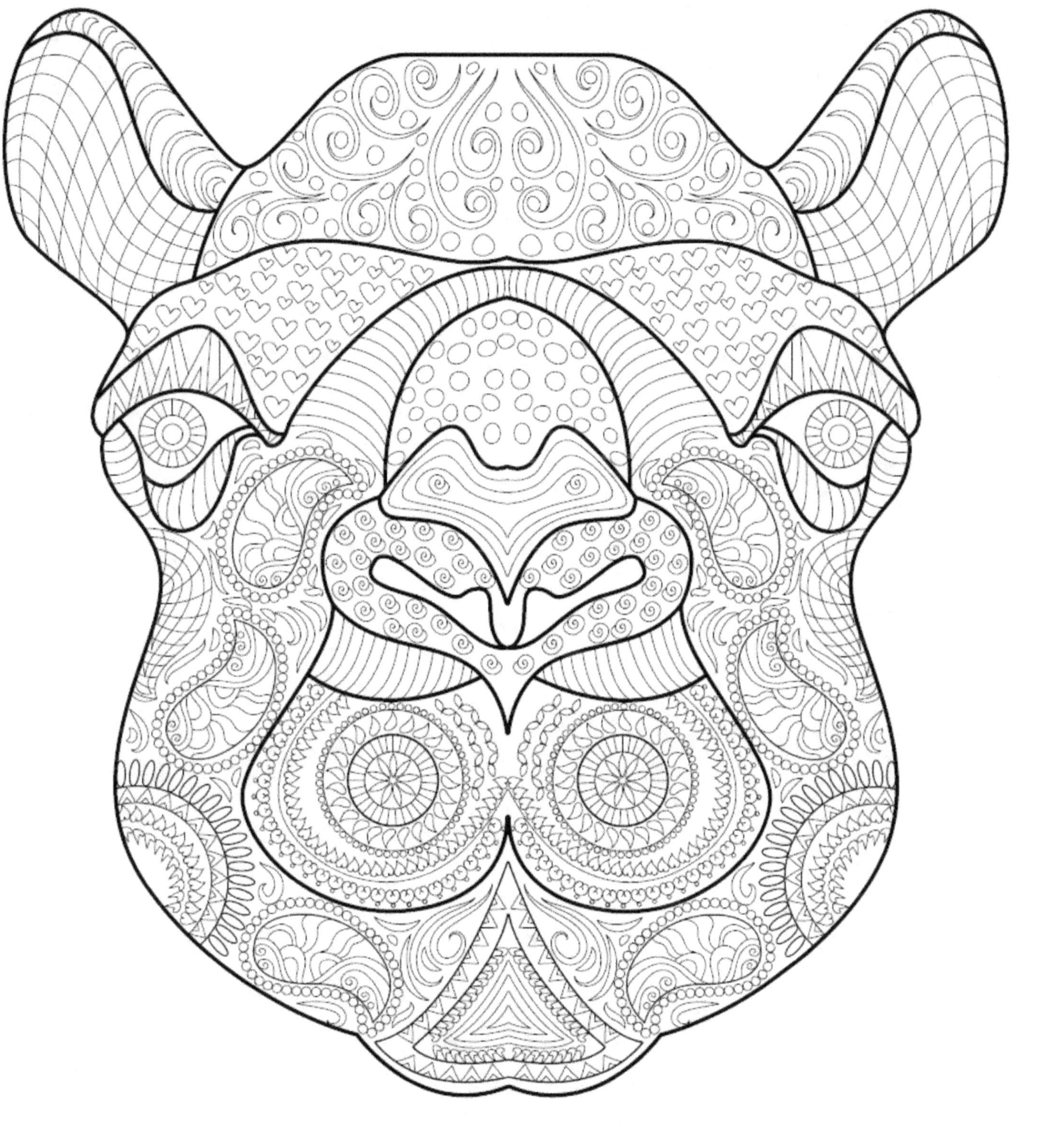

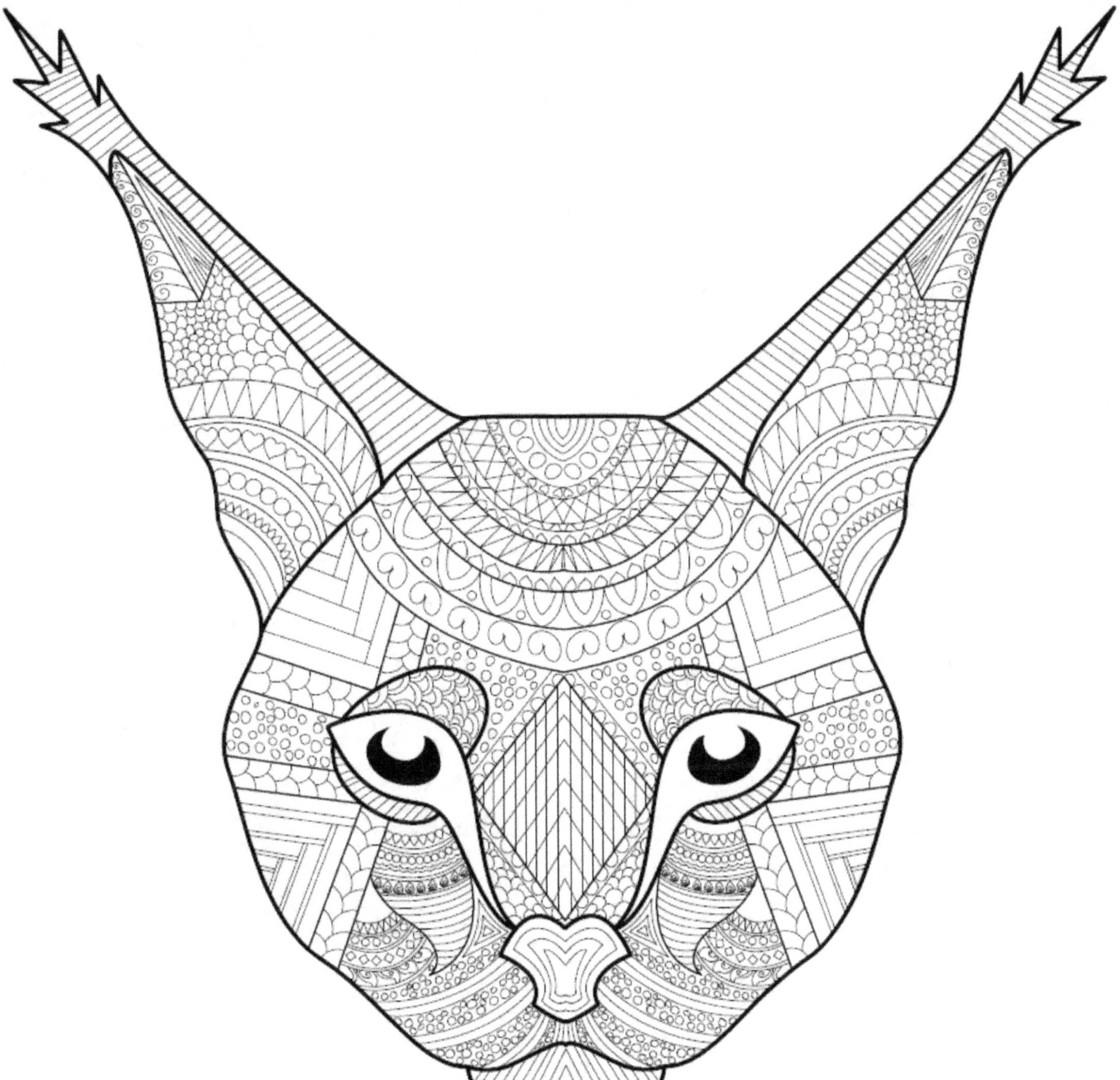

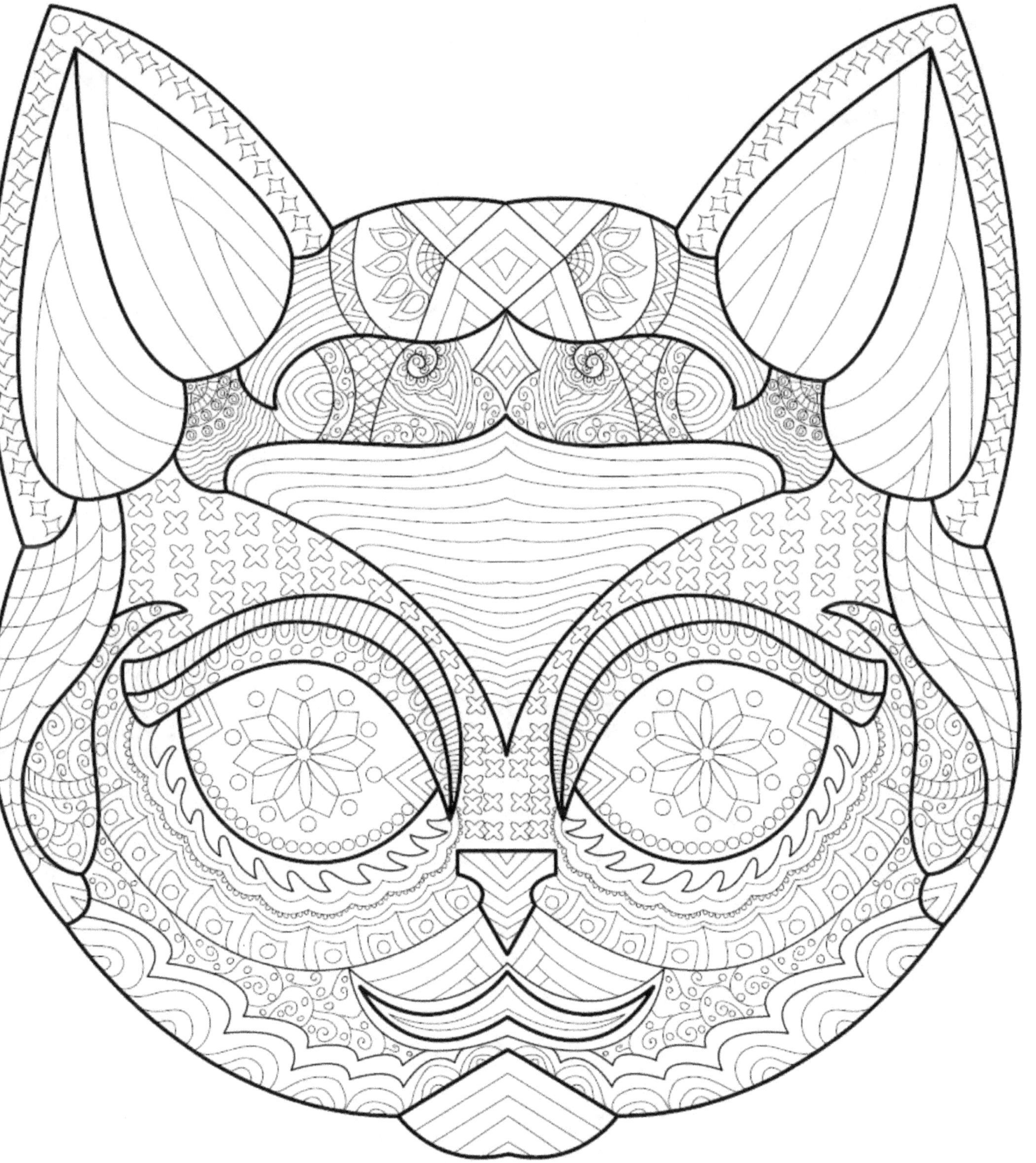

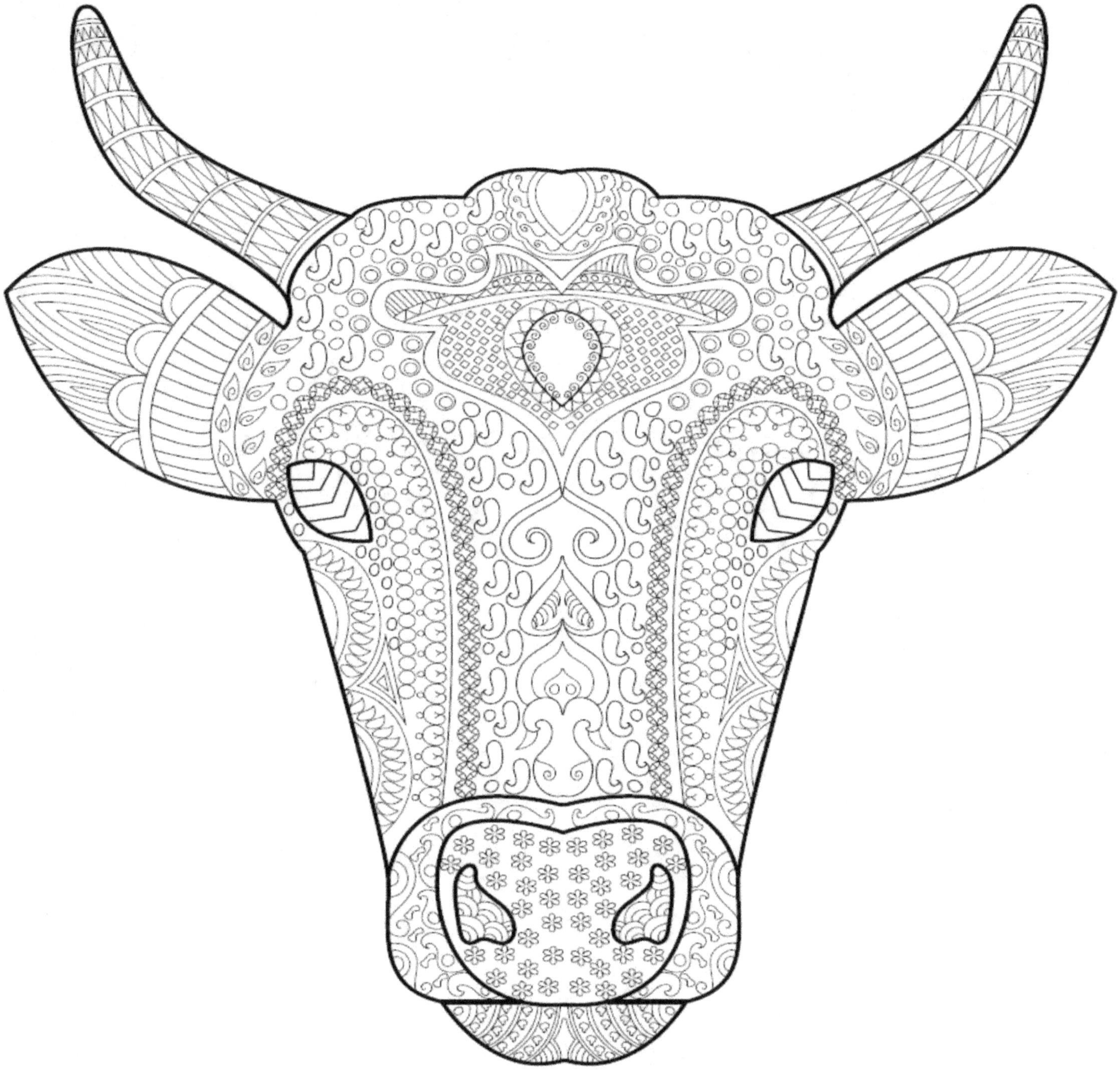

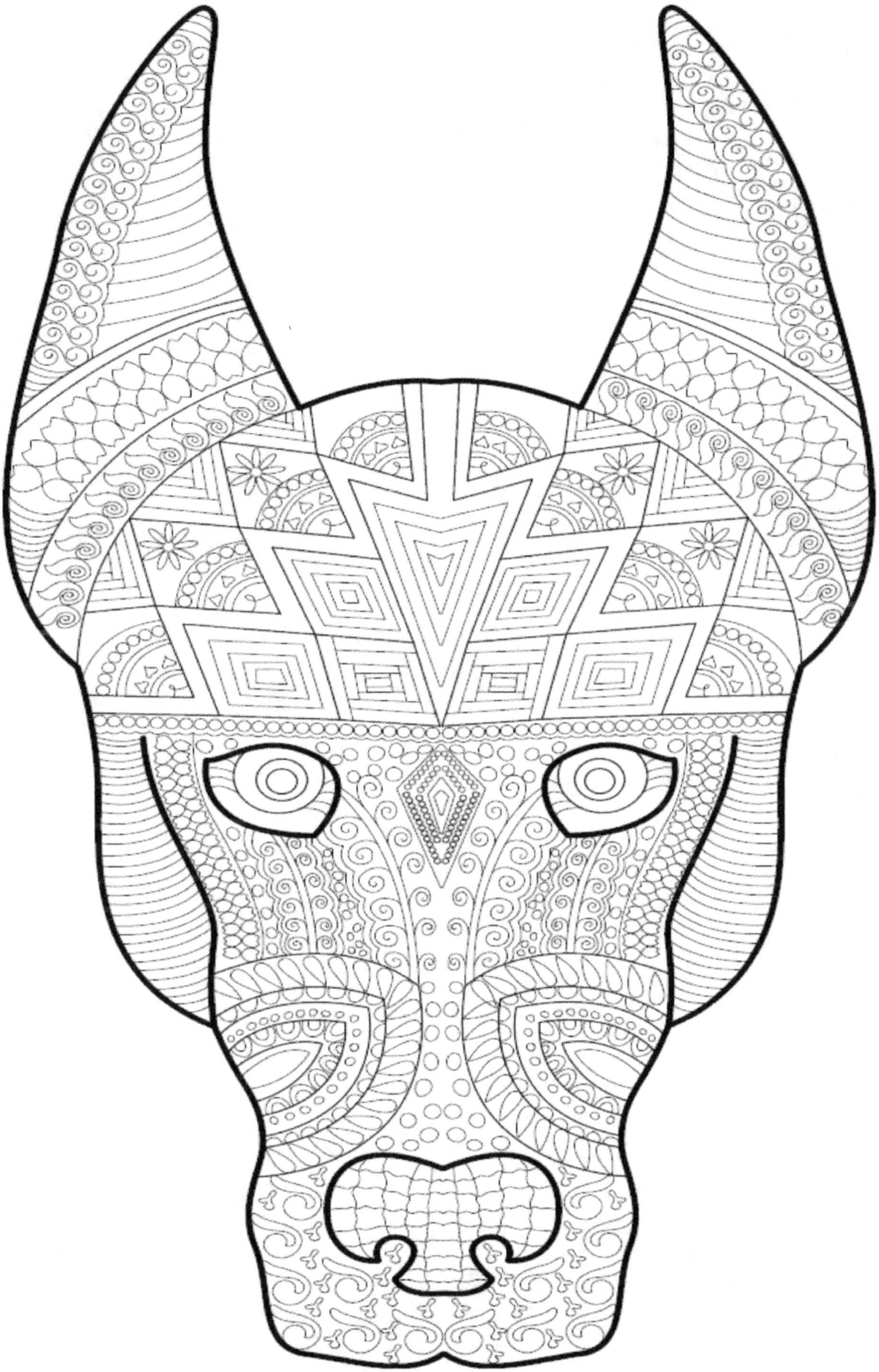

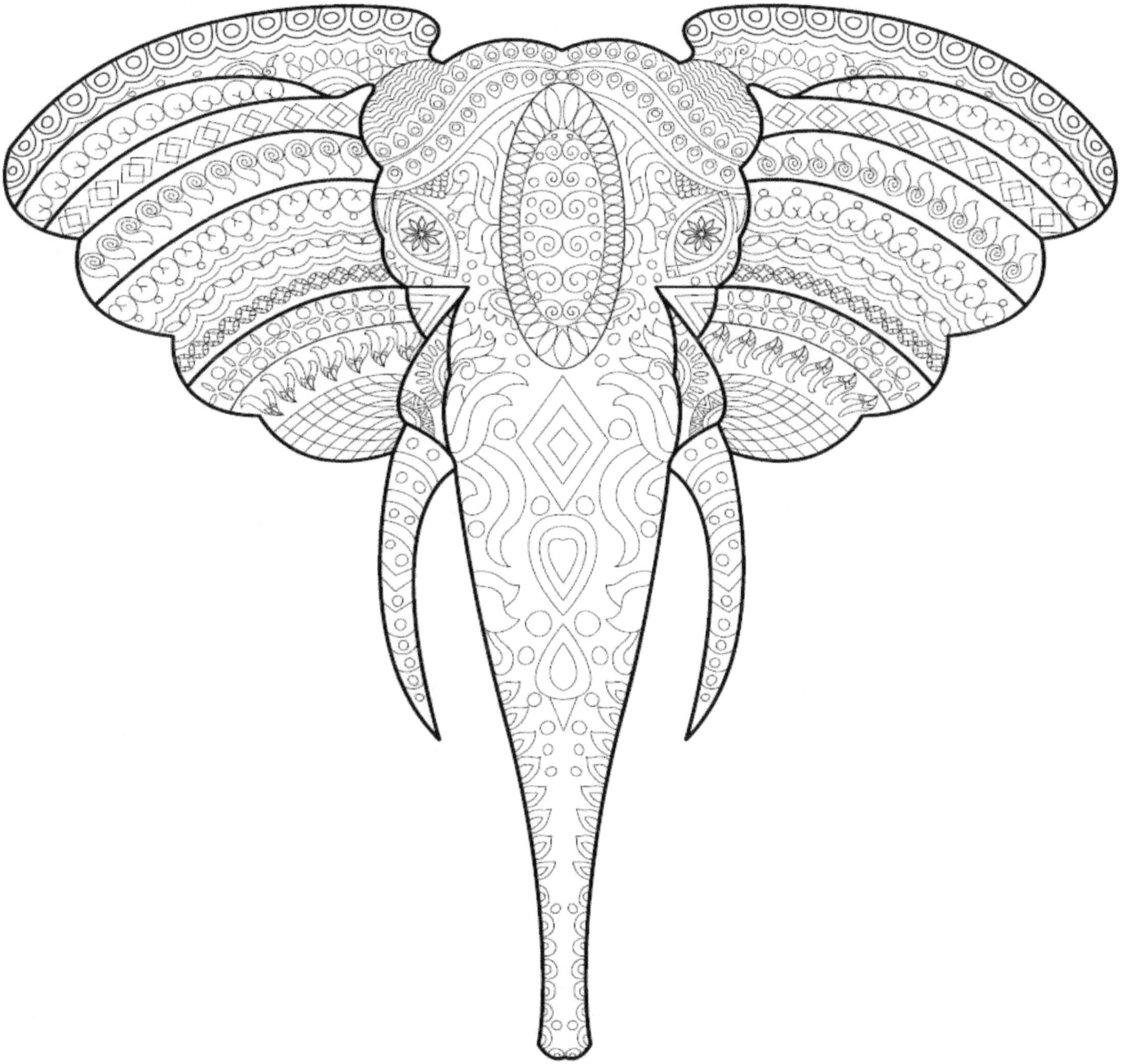

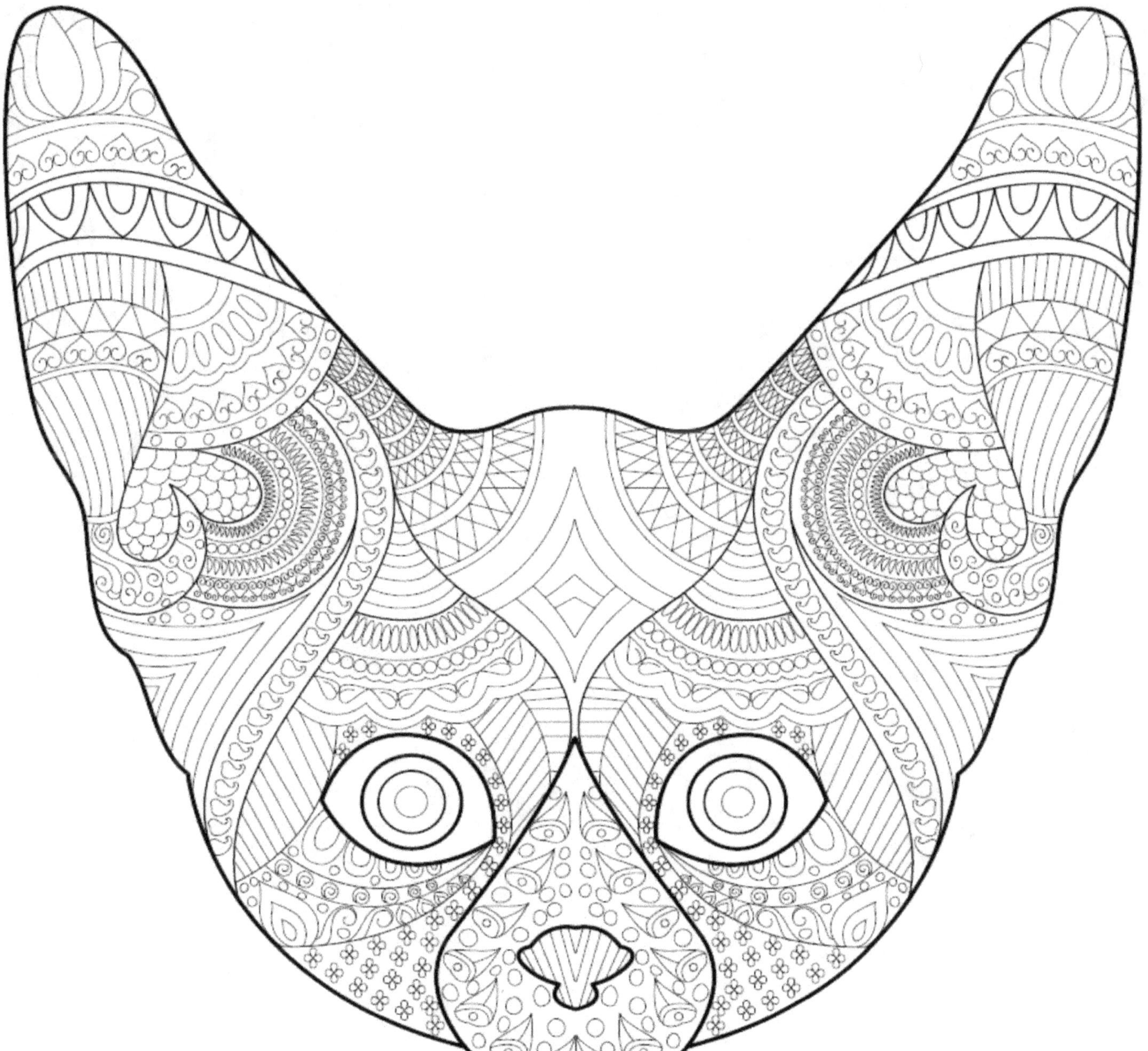

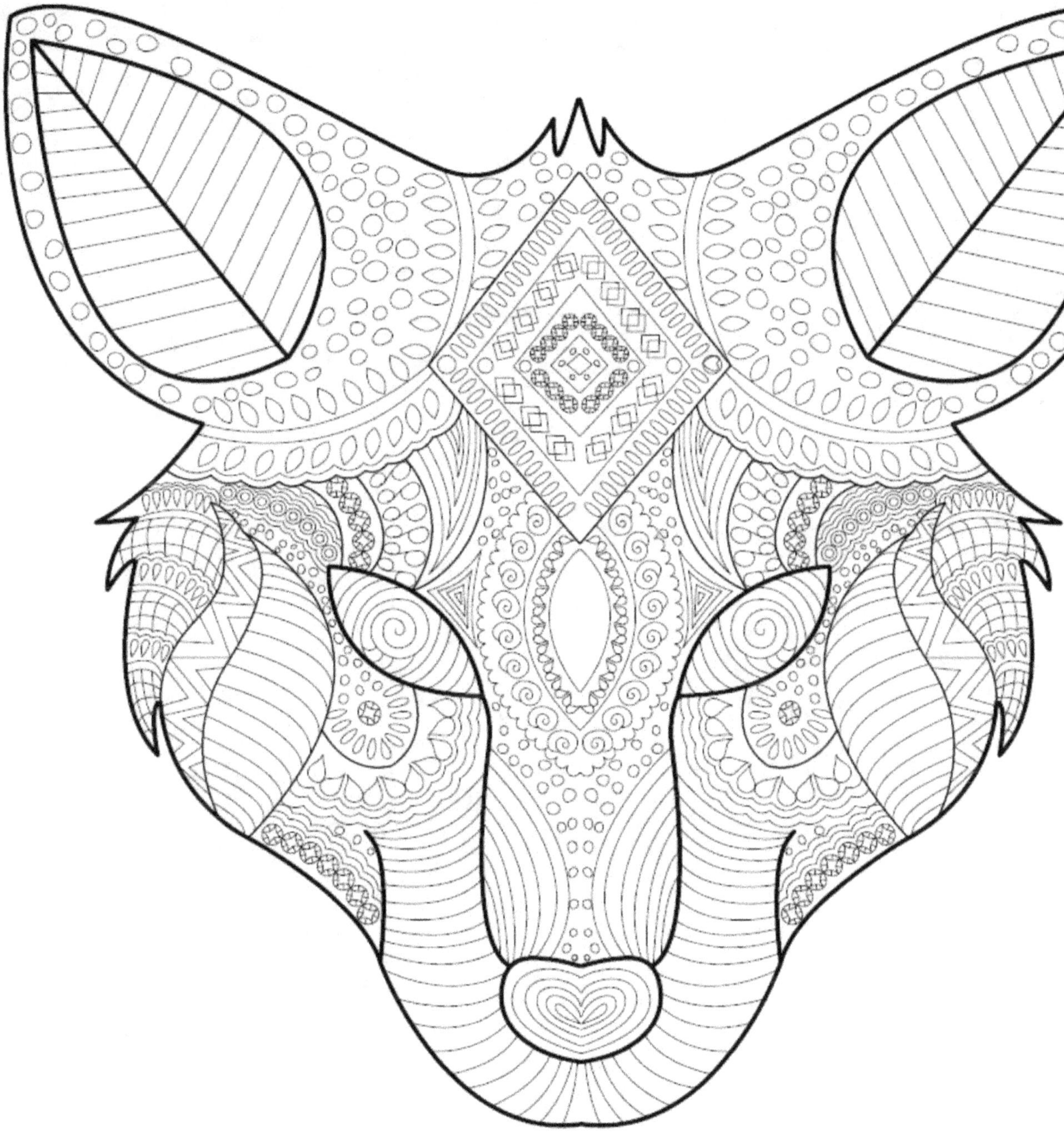

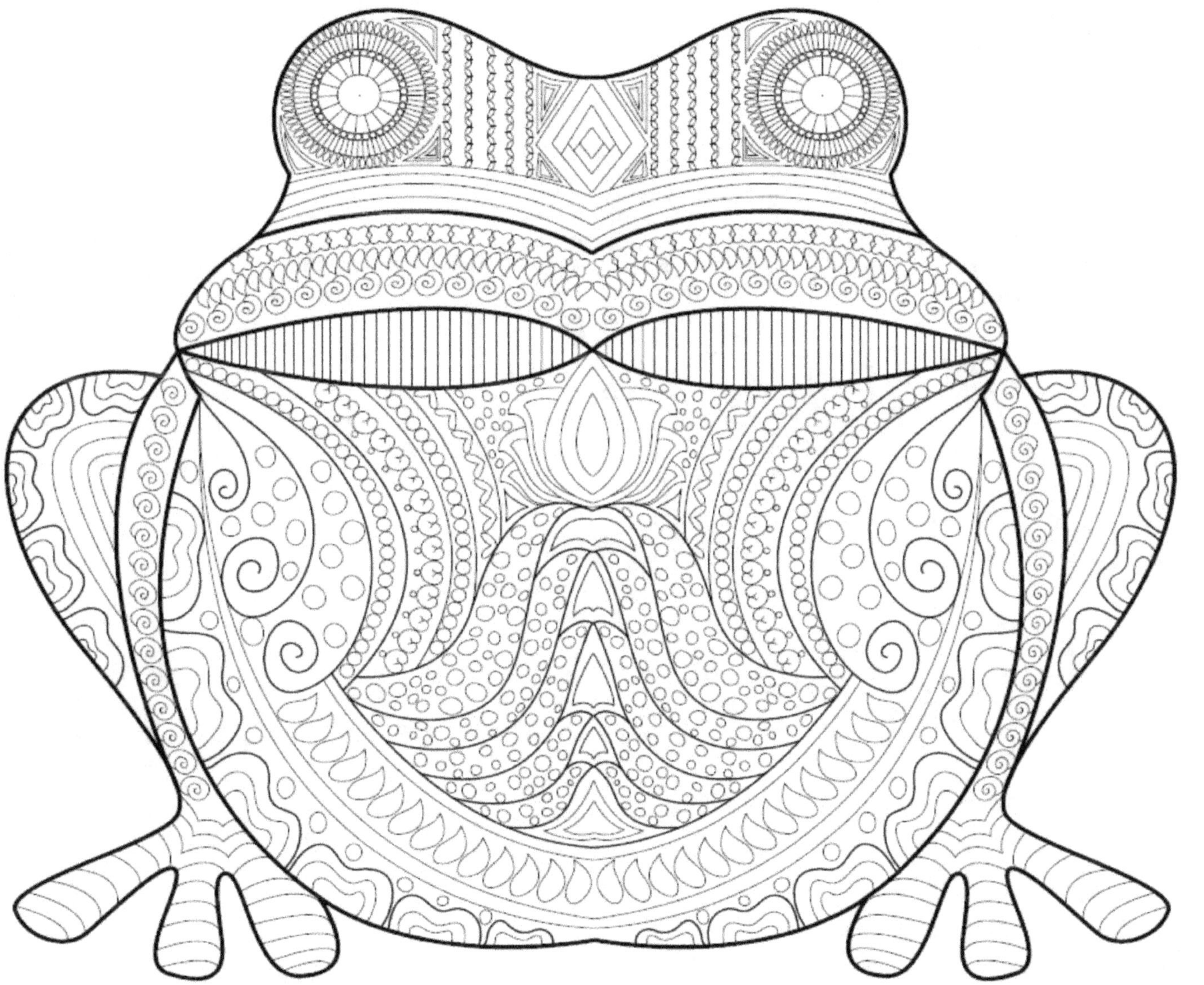

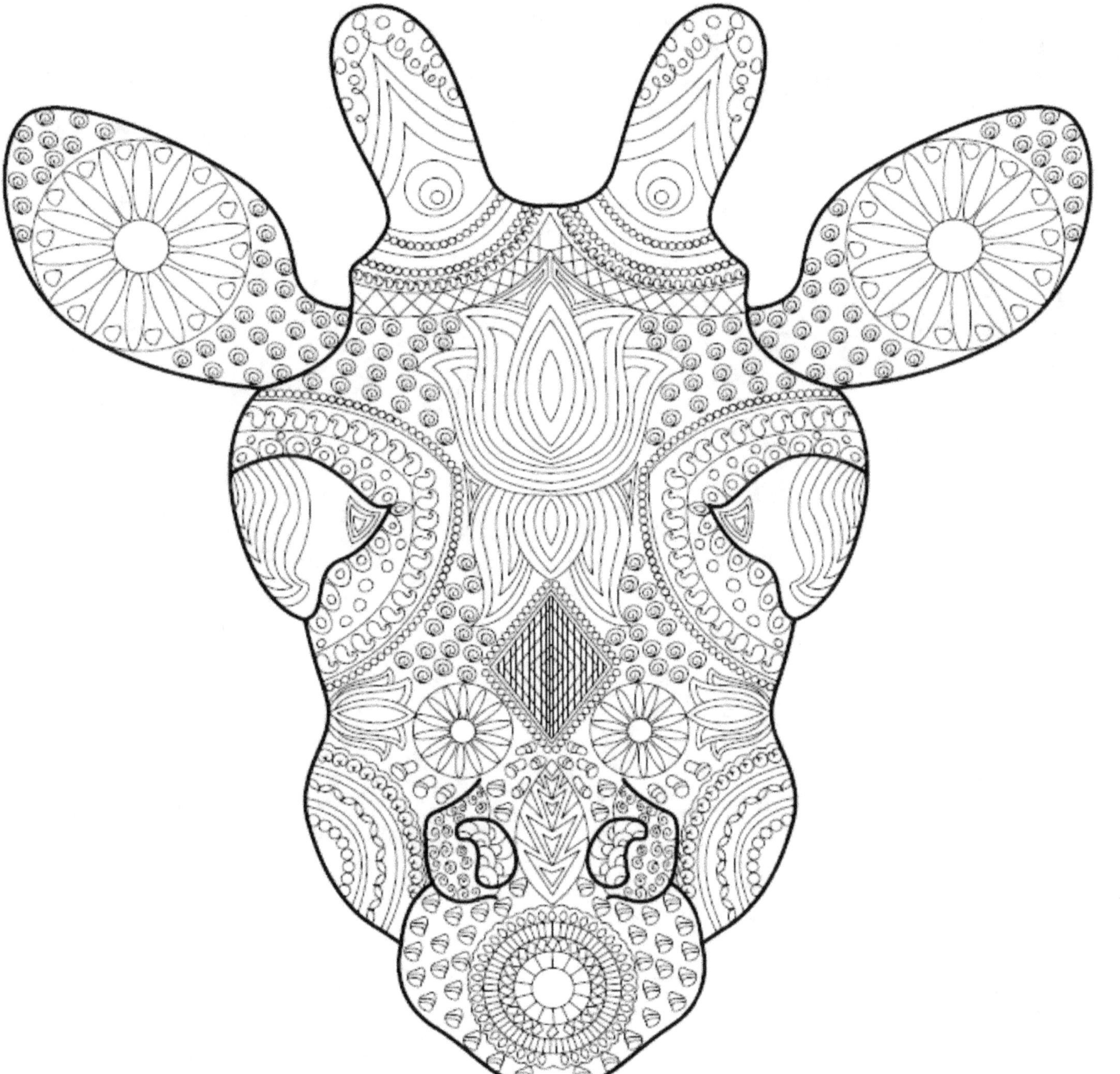

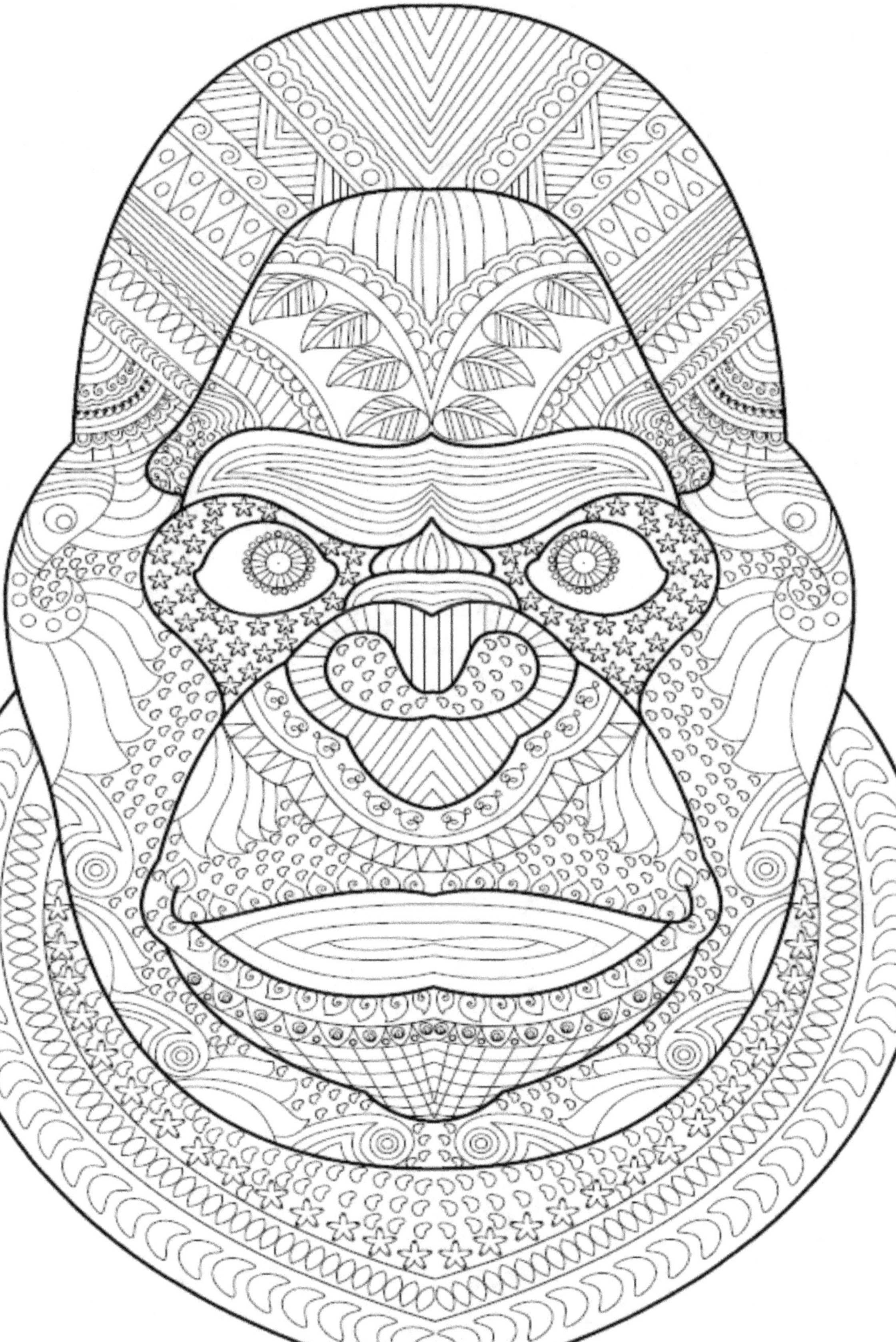

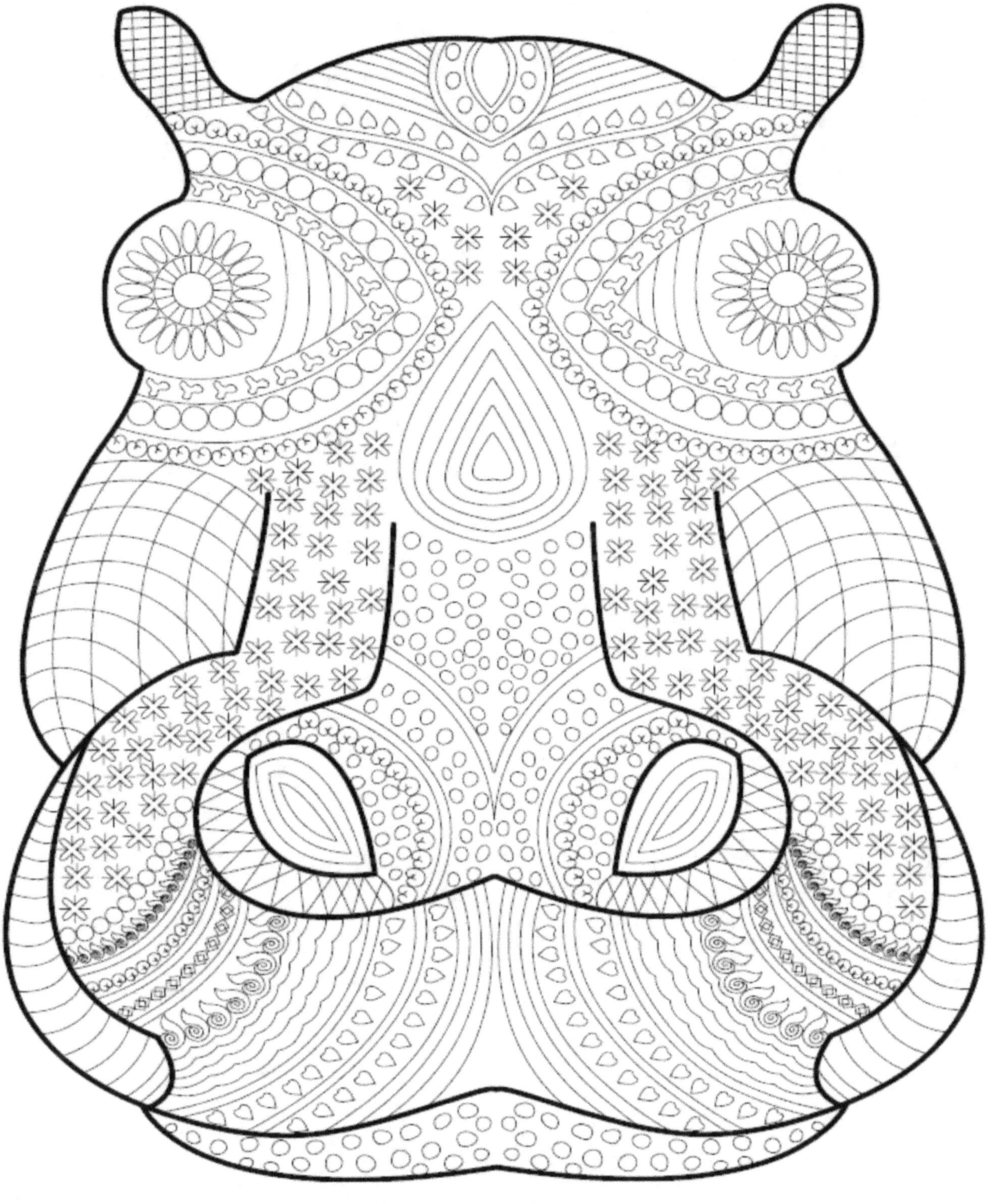

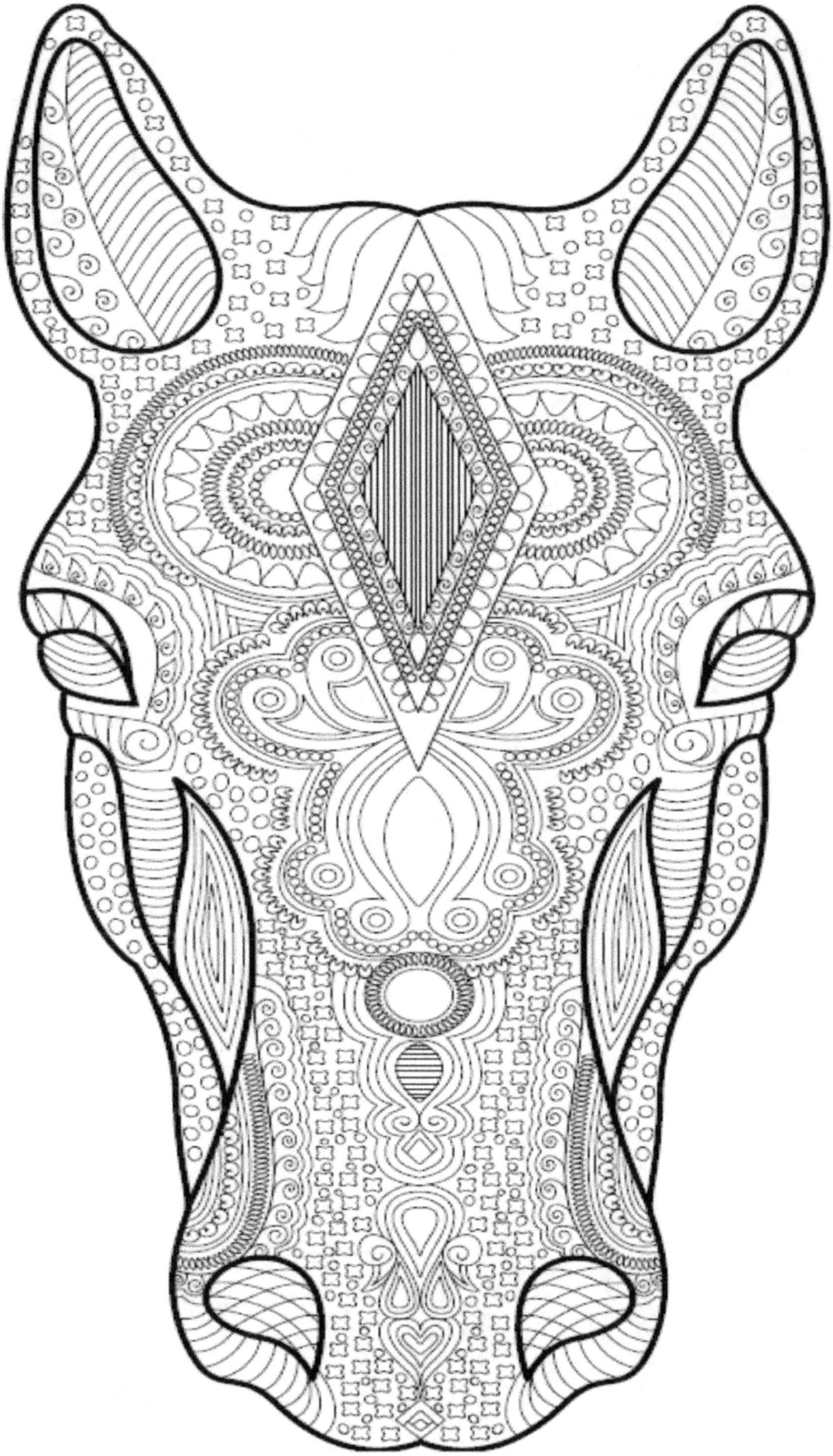

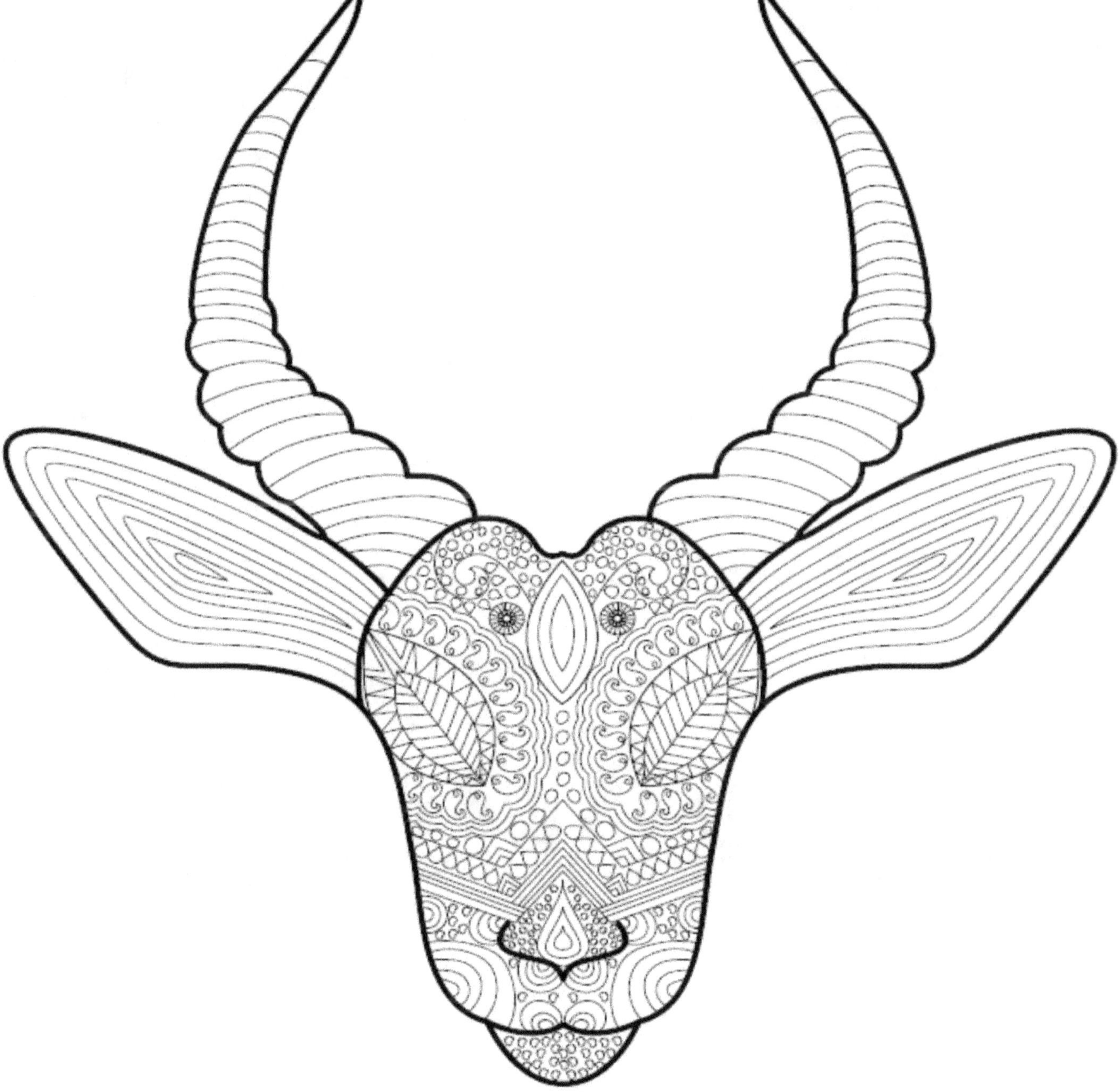

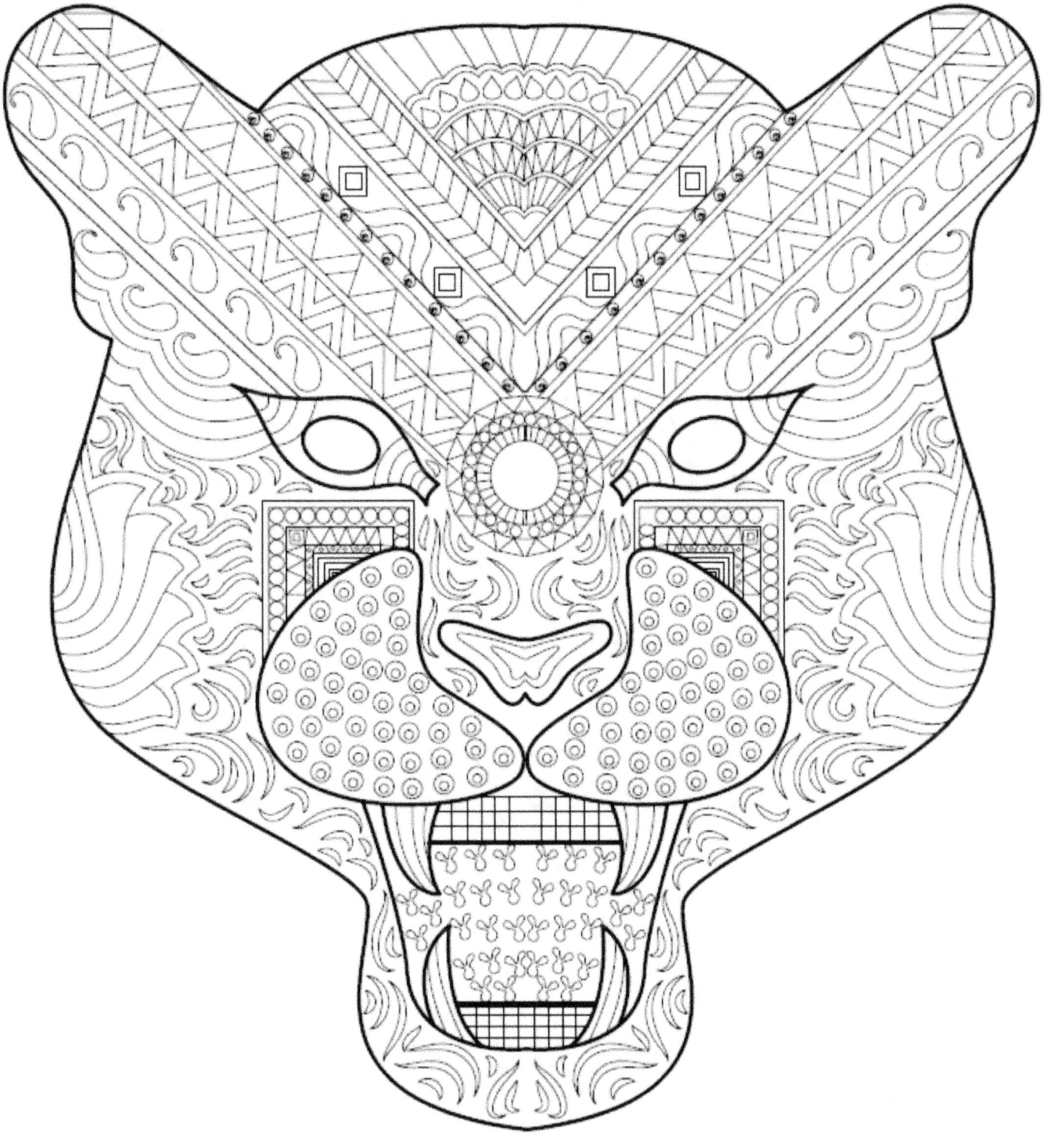

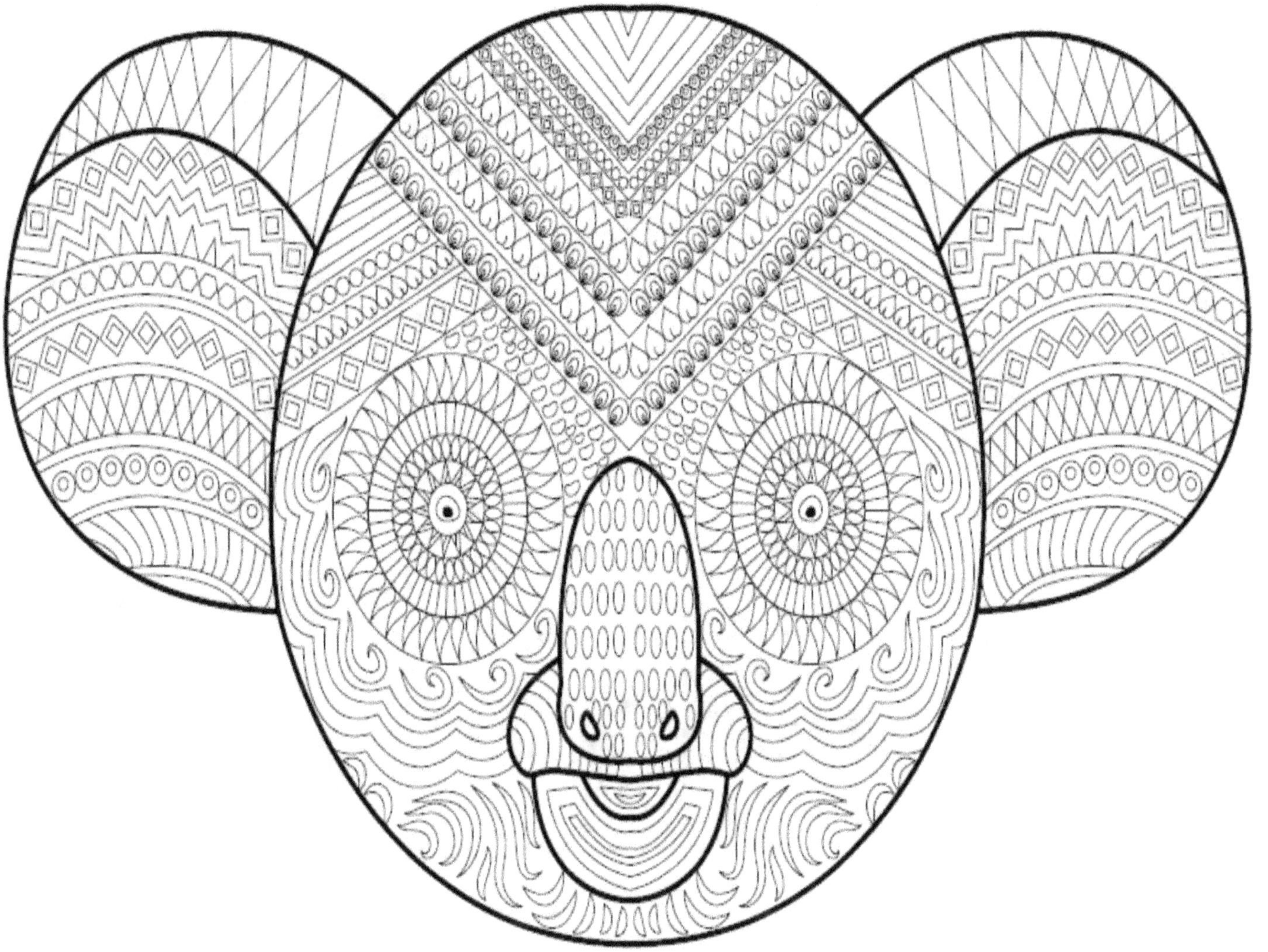

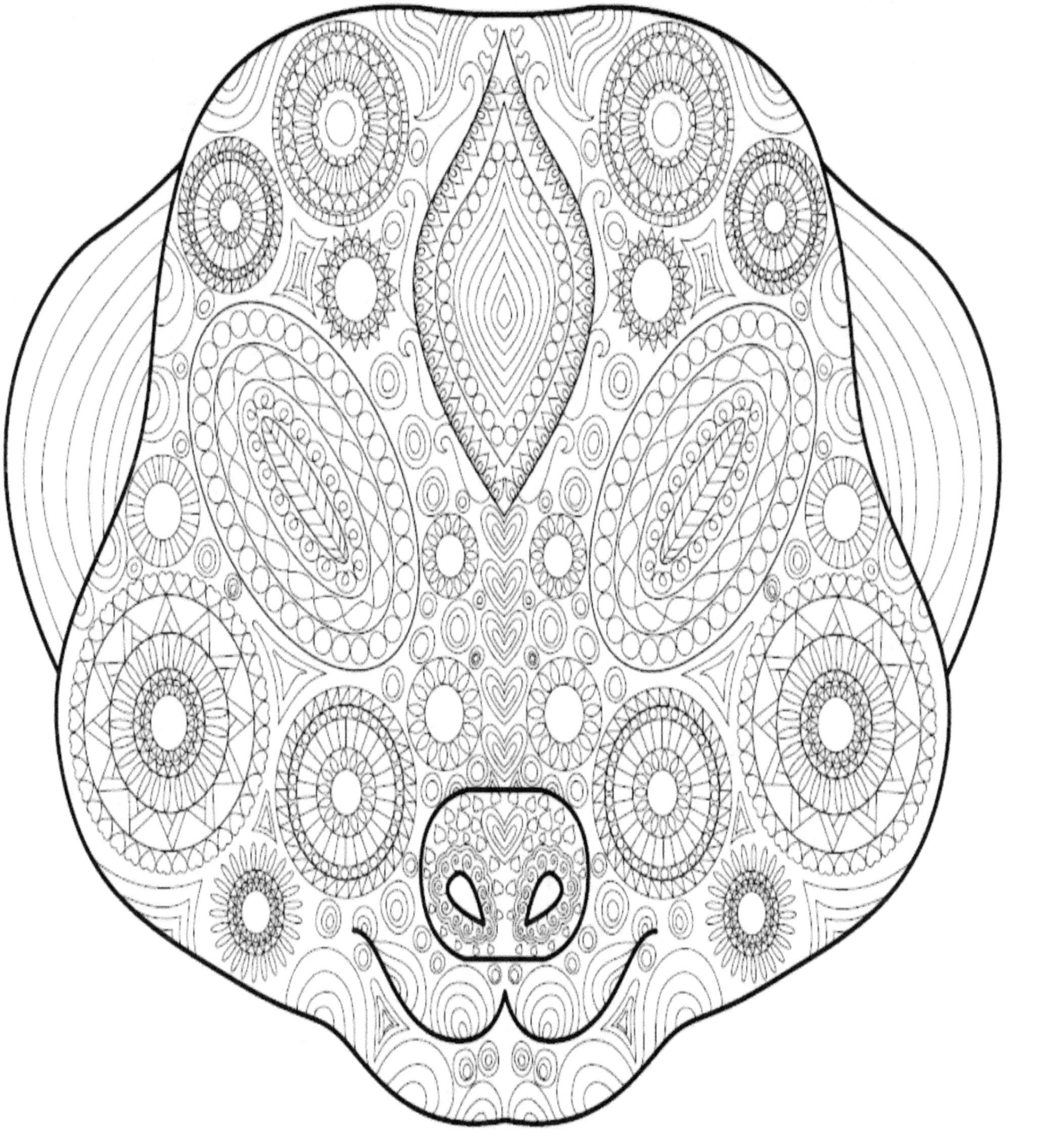

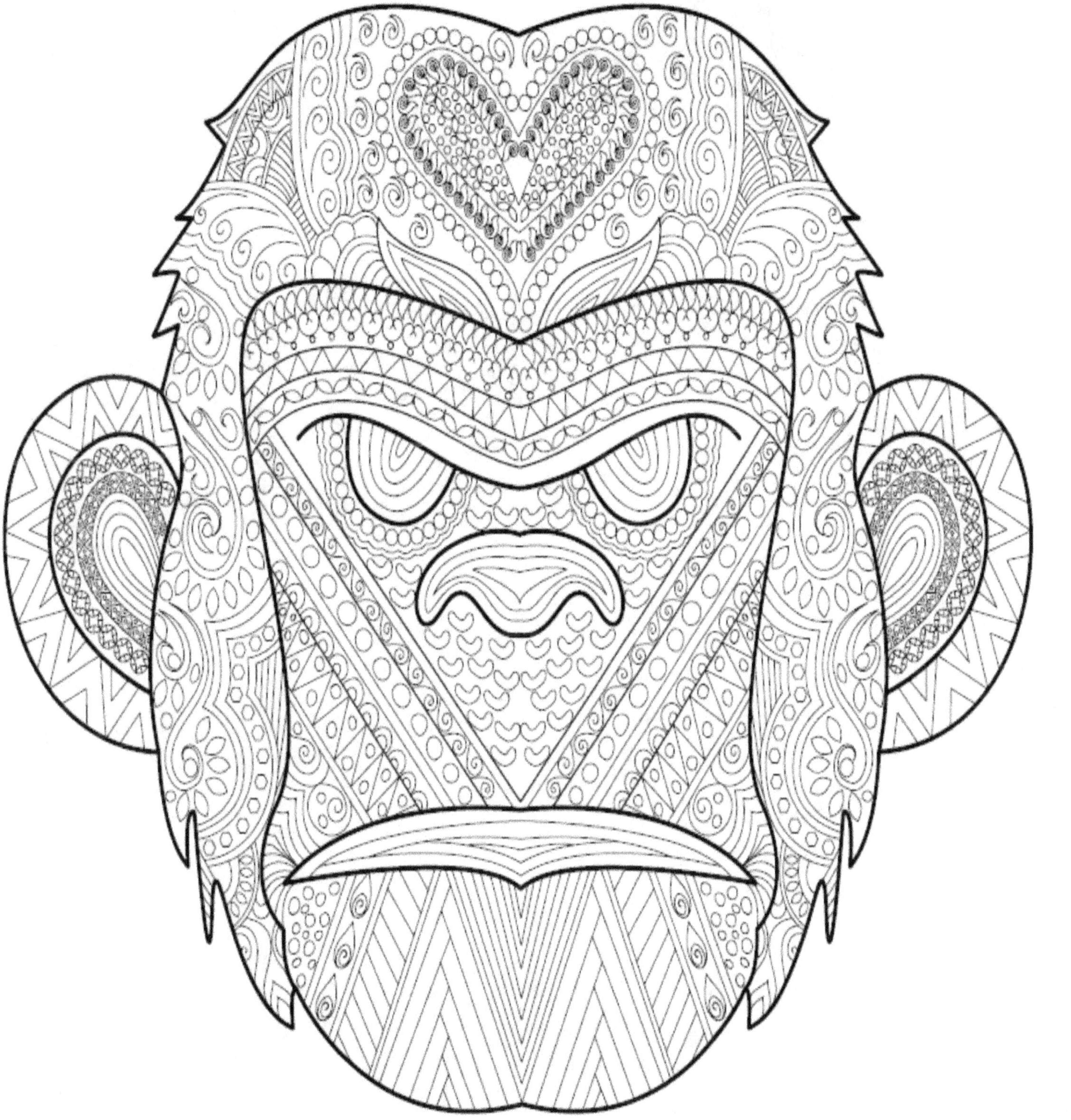

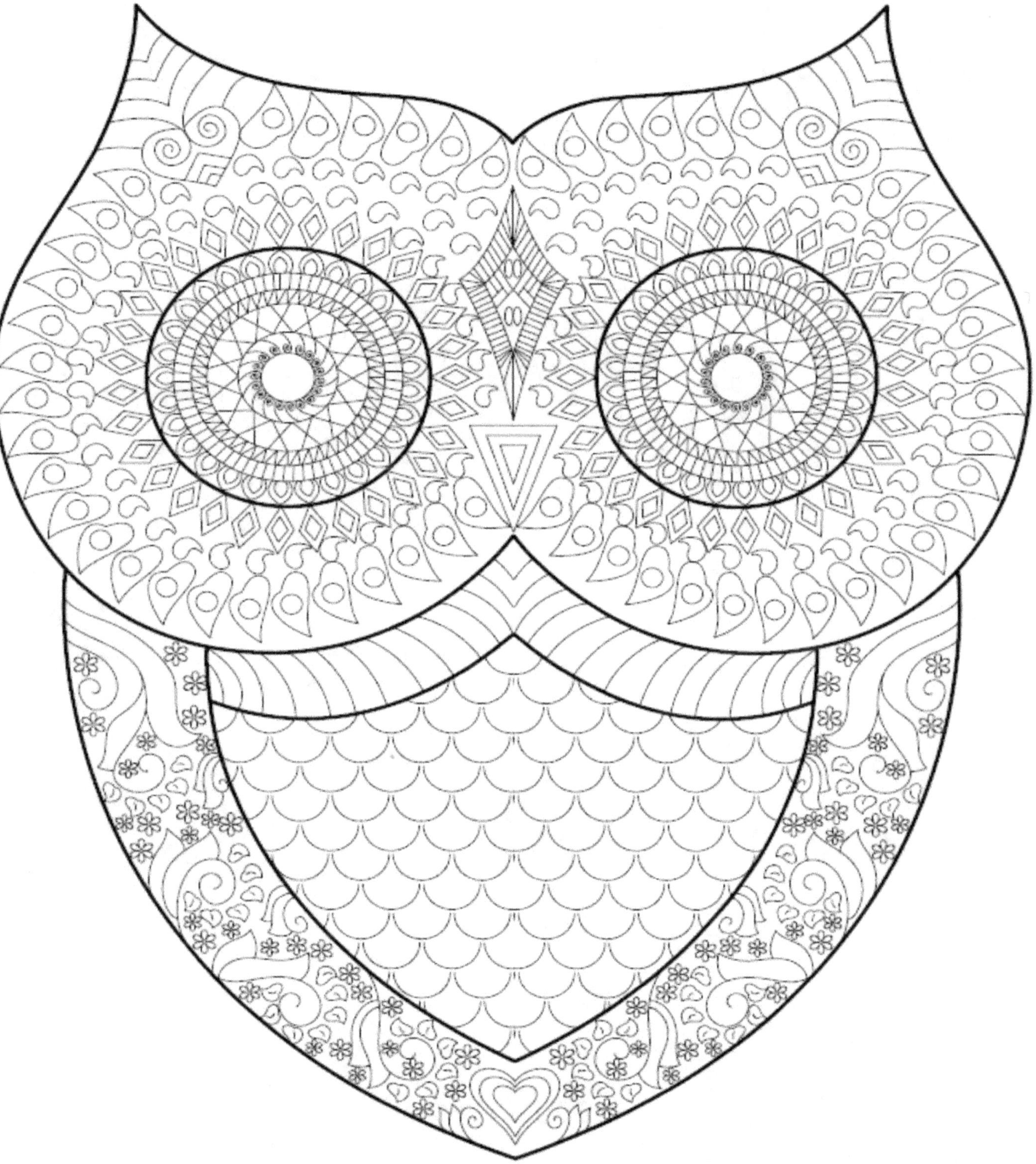

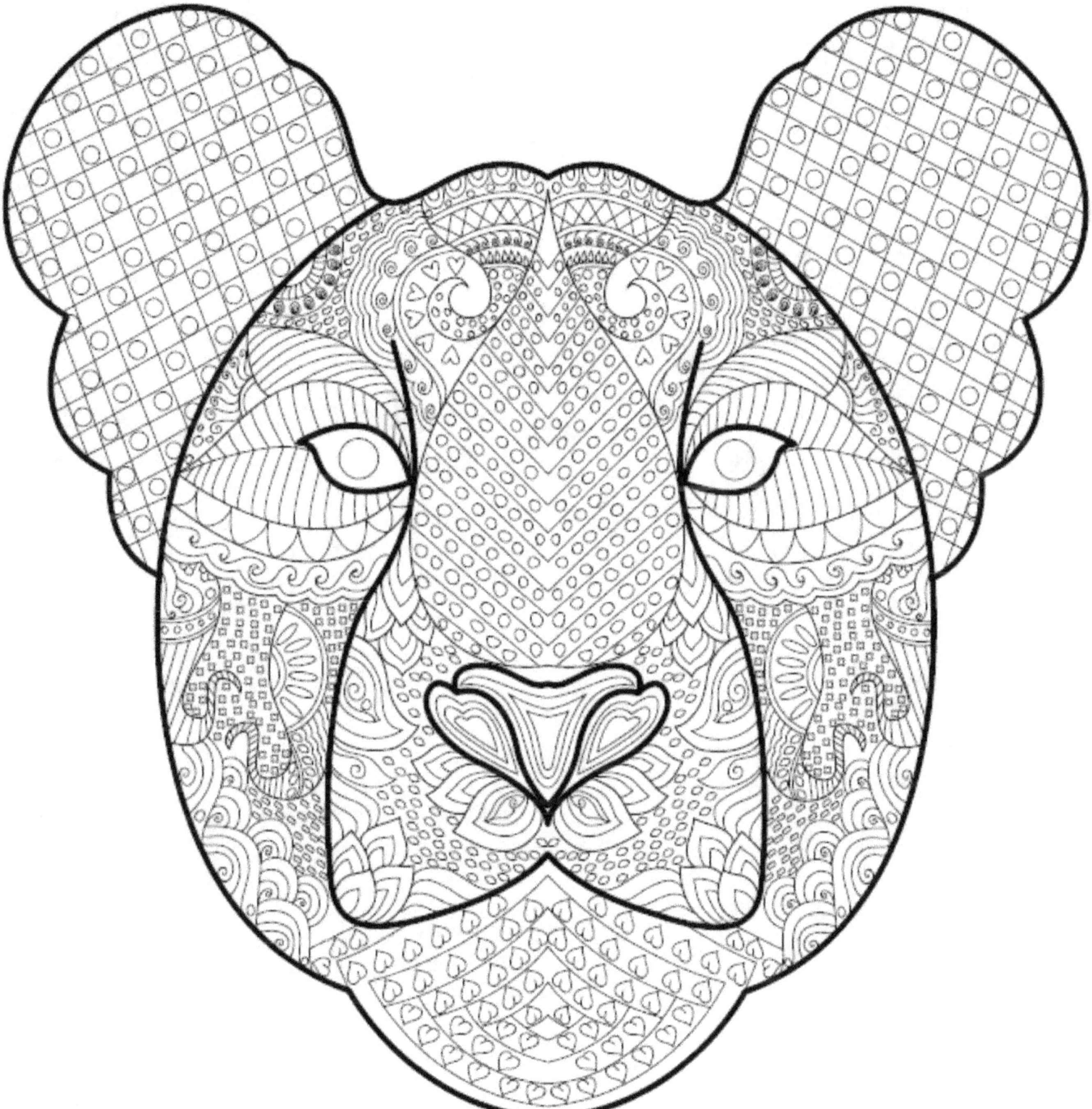

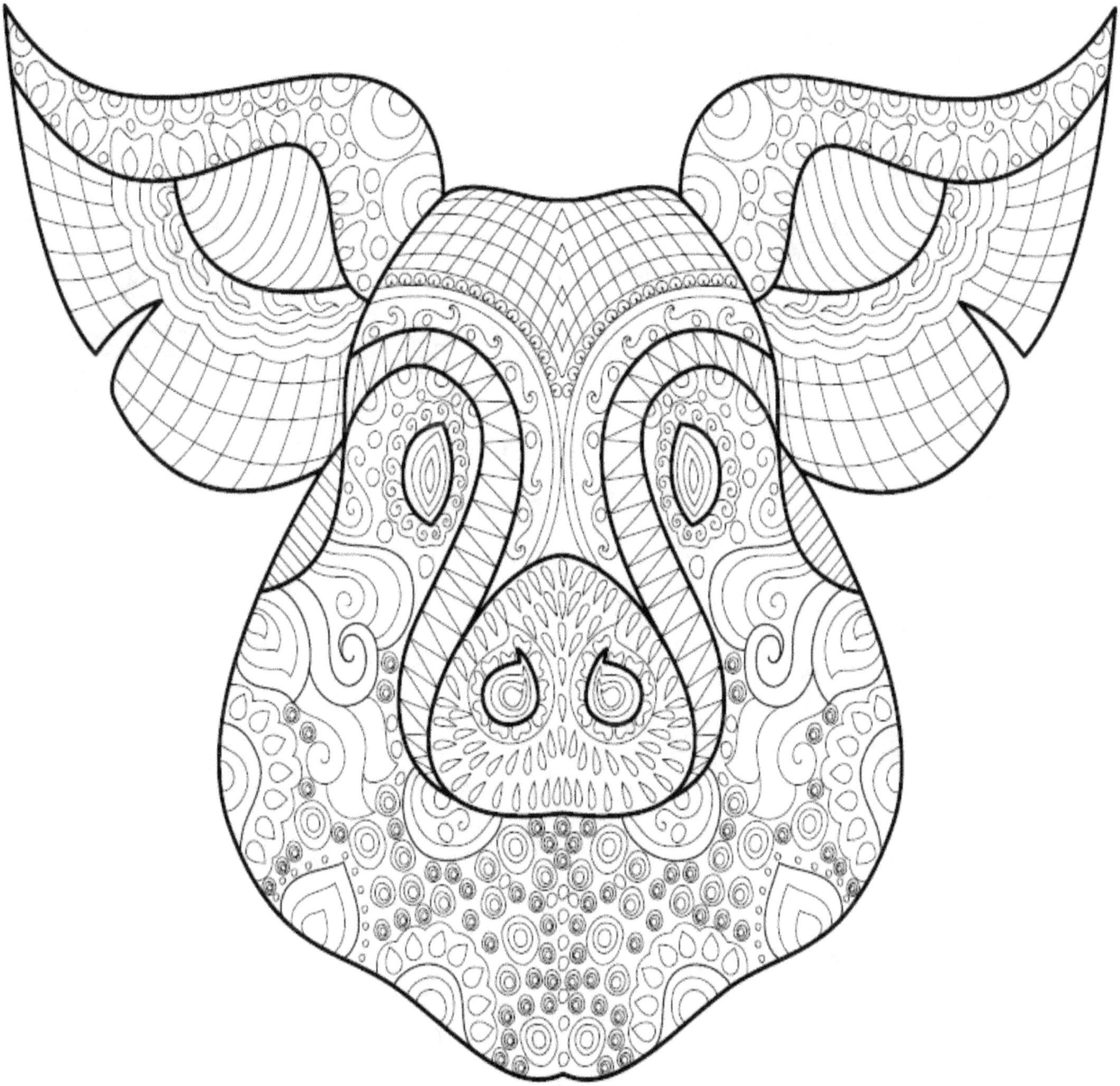

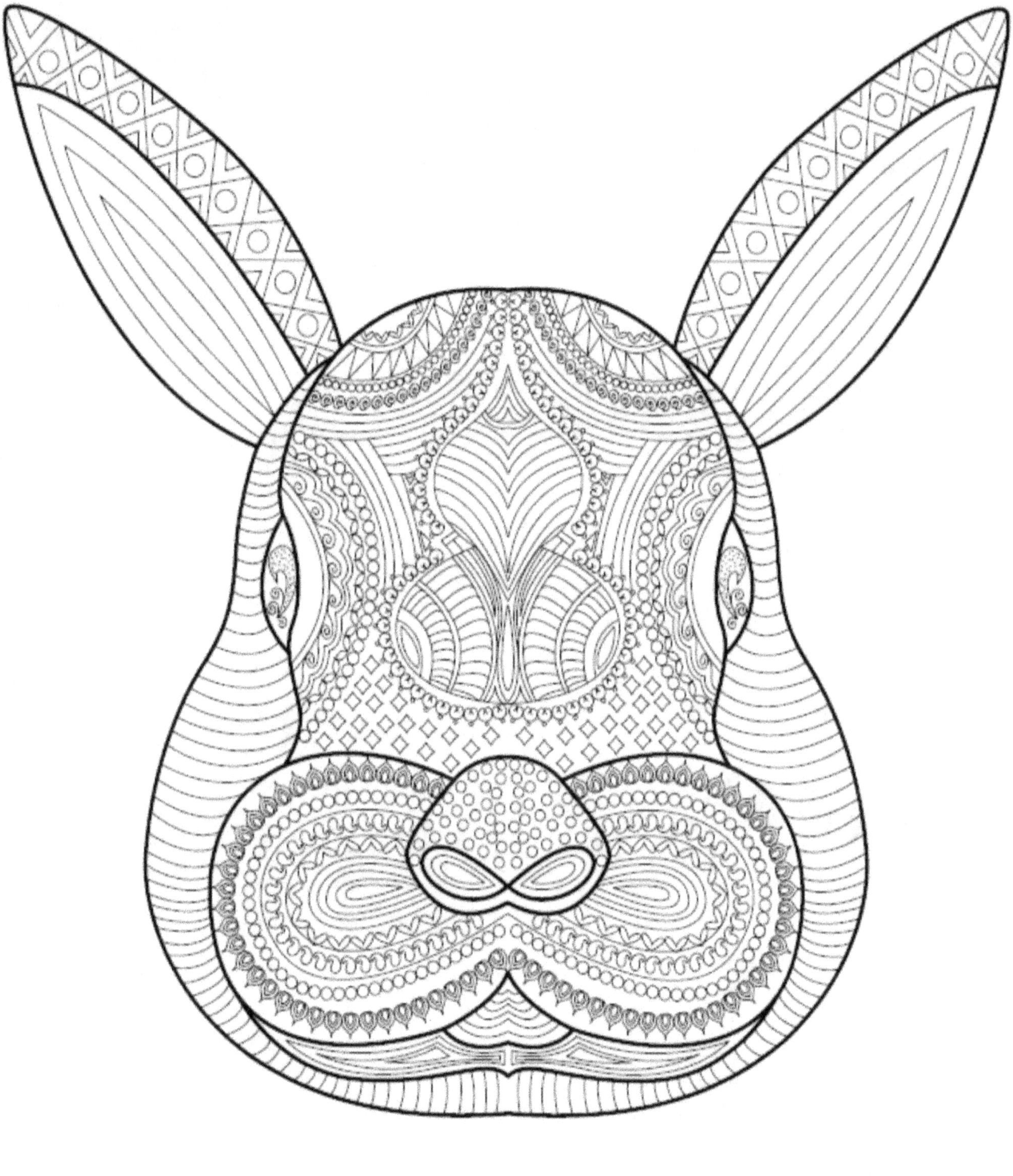

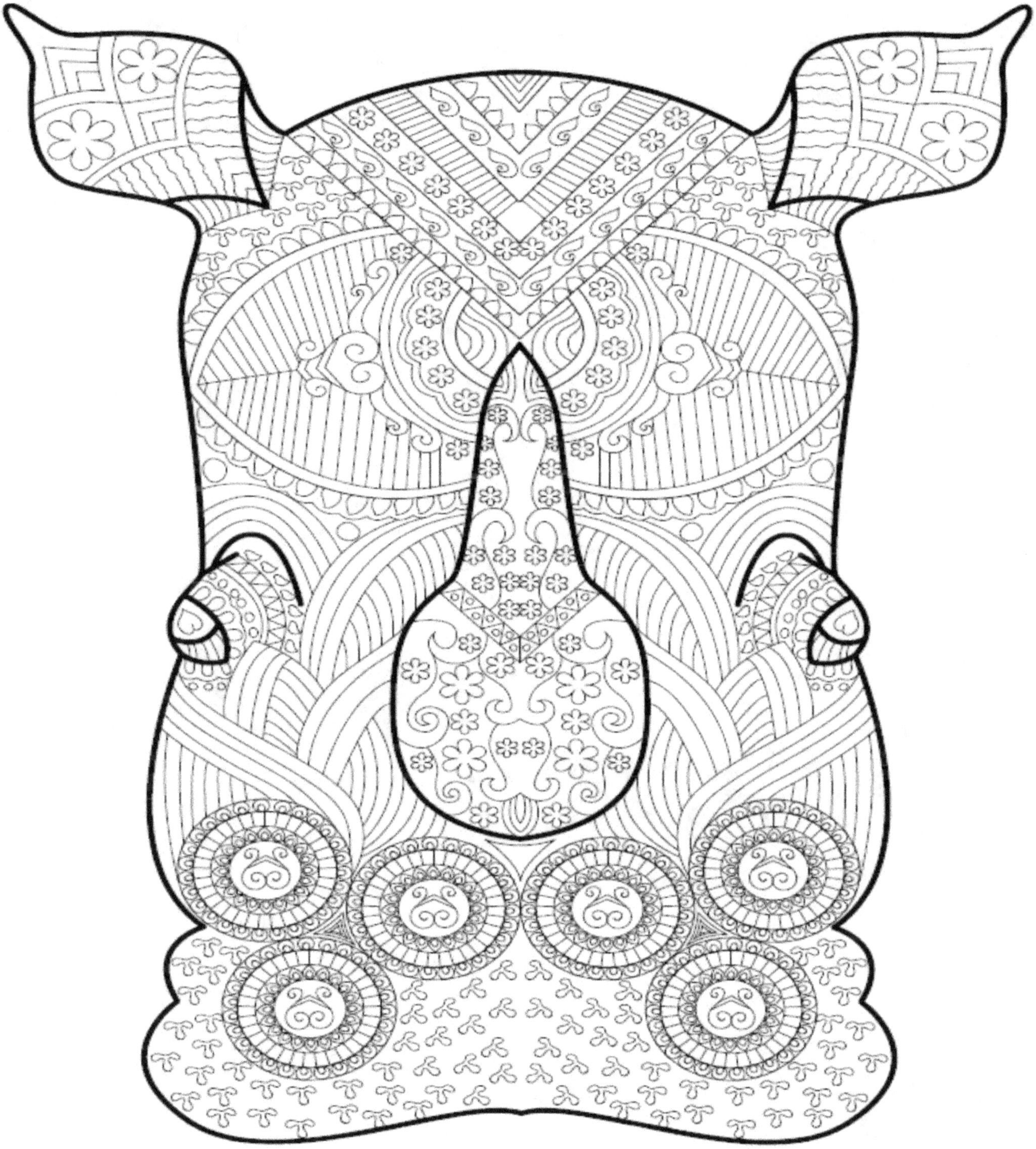

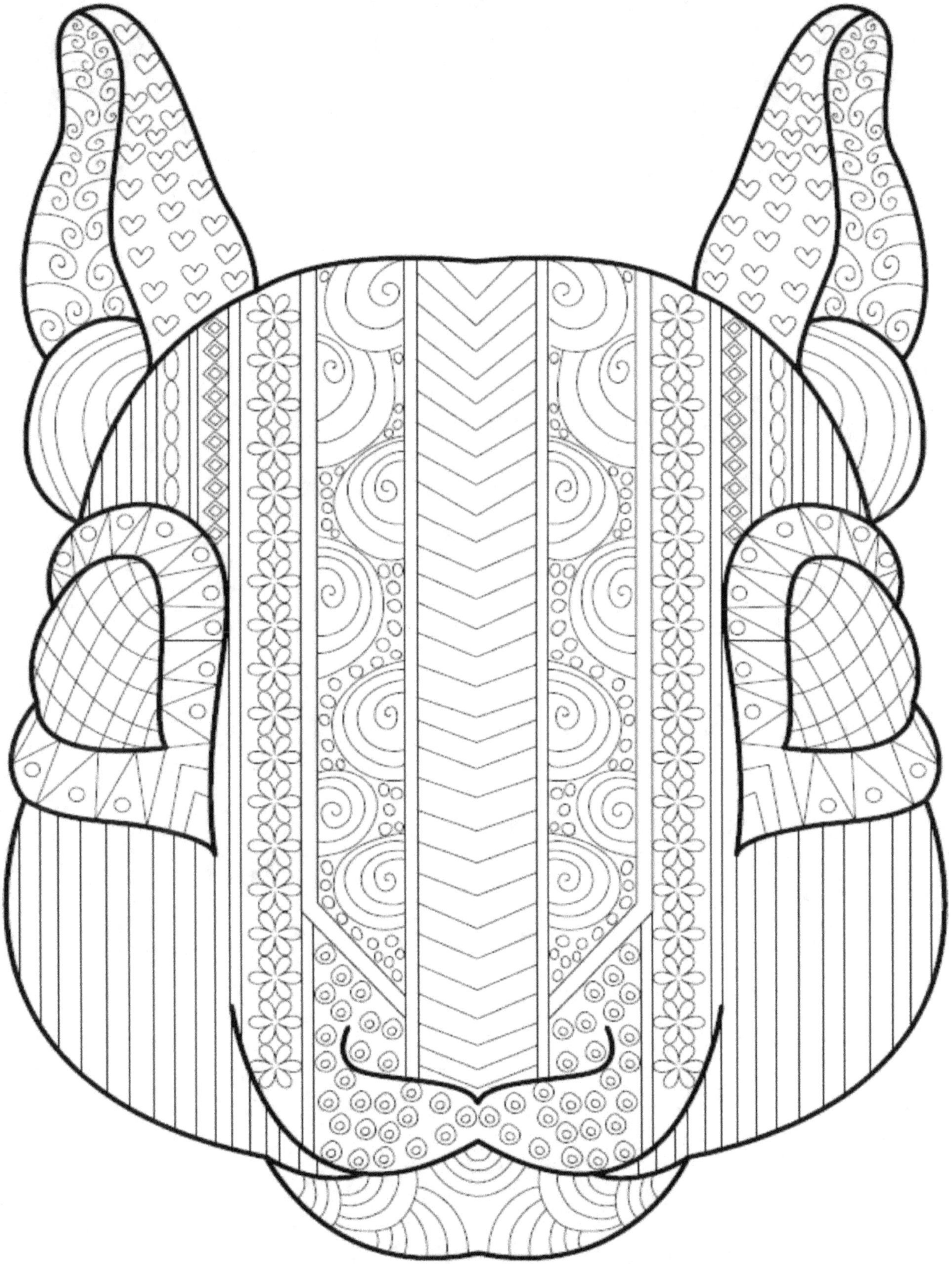

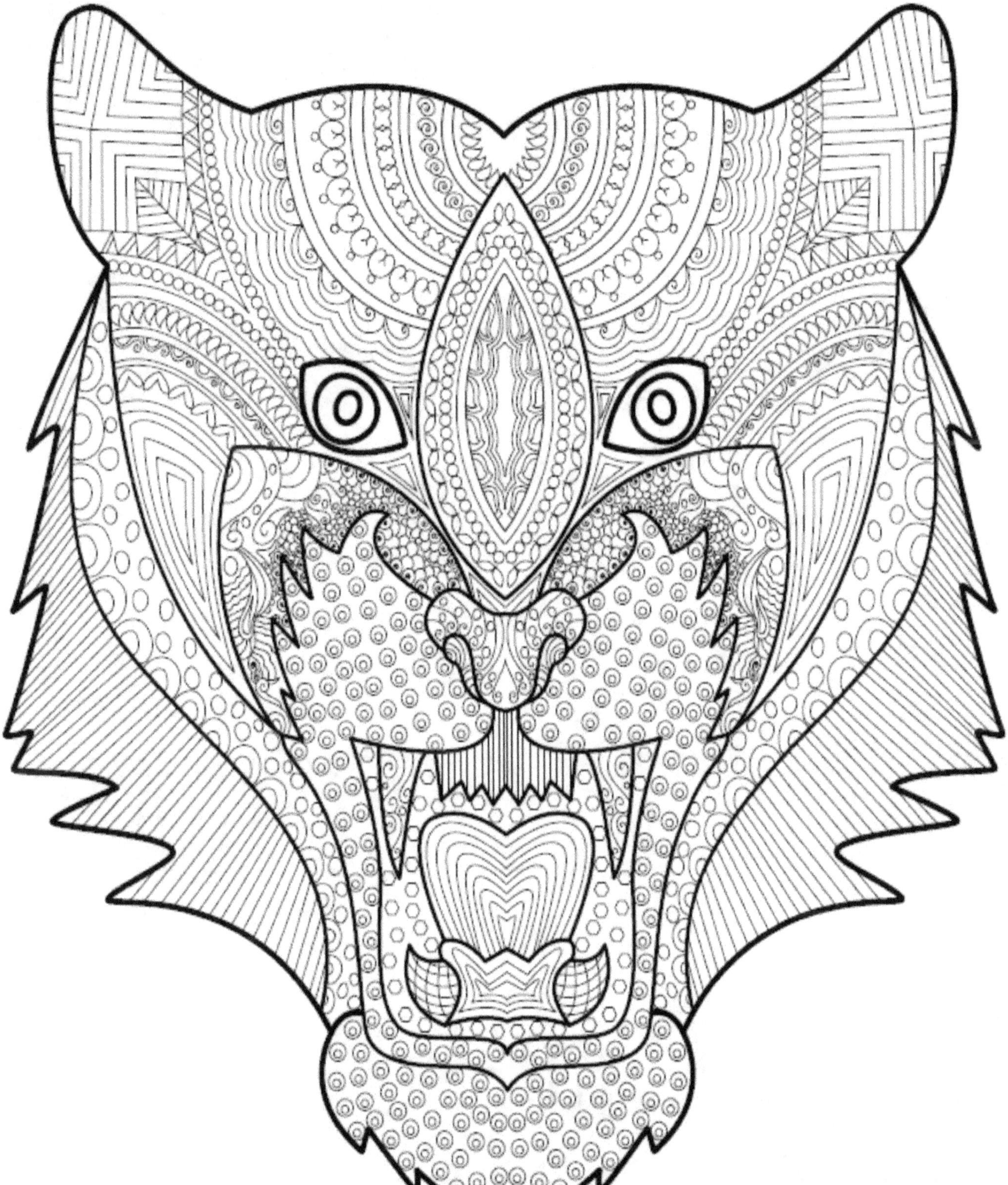

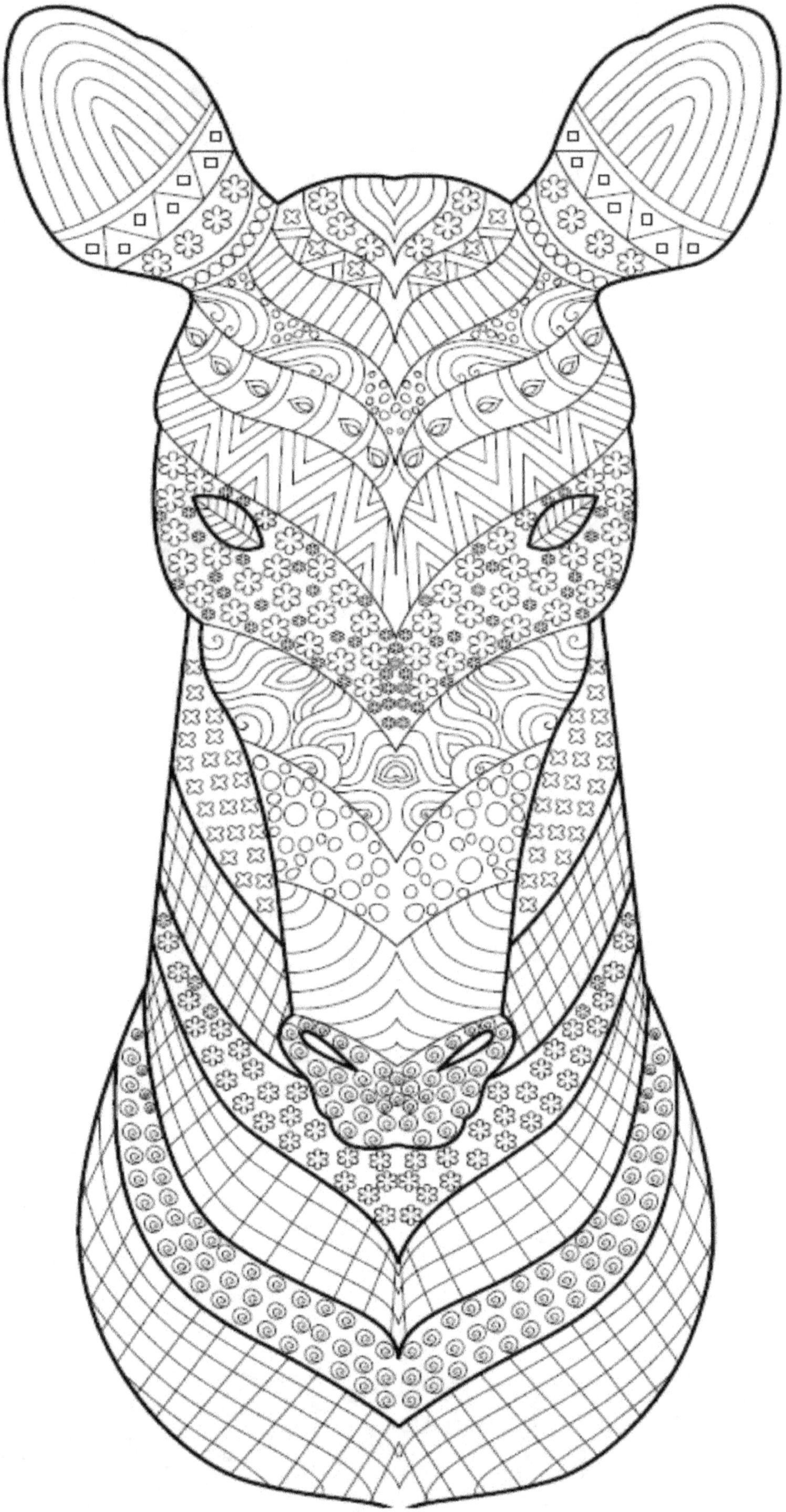

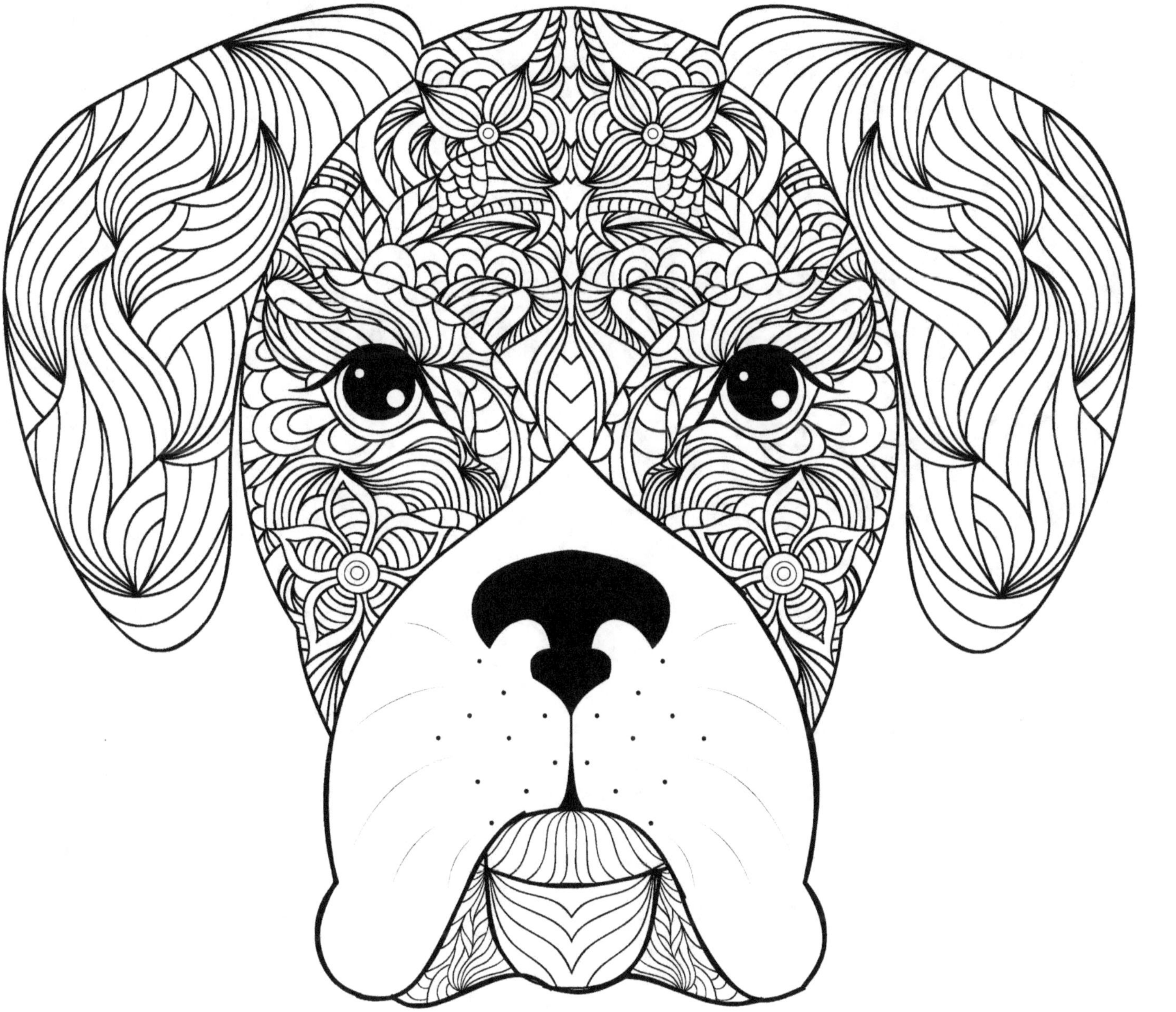

www.ingramcontent.com/pod-product-compliance
Lightning Source LLC
Chambersburg PA
CBHW080833170526
45158CB00009B/2559